The Gospel according to Harry Potter

Spirituality in the Stories of the World's Most Famous Seeker

Connie Neal

 WESTMINSTER
JOHN KNOX PRESS
LOUISVILLE • KENTUCKY

Book design by Sharon Adams
Cover illustration by Teri Vinson

First edition
Published by Westminster John Knox Press
Louisville, Kentucky

This book is printed on acid-free paper that meets the American National Standards Institute Z39.48 standard. ♾

PRINTED IN THE UNITED STATES OF AMERICA

05 06 07 08 09 10 11 — 10 9 8 7 6 5

Library of Congress Cataloging-in-Publication Data

Neal, C. W. (Connie W.), date
The Gospel according to Harry Potter : spirituality in the stories of the world's most famous seeker / by Connie Neal.— 1st ed.
p. cm.
ISBN 0-664-22601-9 (alk. paper)
1. Rowling, J. K.—Religion. 2. Christian fiction, English—History and criticism. 3. Children's stories, English—History and criticism. 4. Fantasy fiction, English—History and criticism. 5. Rowling, J. K.—Characters—Harry Potter. 6. Potter, Harry (Fictitious character) 7. Spirituality in literature. 8. Religion in literature. I. Title.

PR6068.O93 Z78 2002
823.914—dc21

2002069181

For those who have eyes to see

Contents

Introduction

As I write this, I am in my yard on a bright spring day. Overhead, a host of white clouds decorate a brilliant blue sky. On days like this I long to let my gaze linger to see if I can make out shapes in the clouds. This was one of my most pleasant childhood pastimes, as I suppose it has been for children throughout the ages, regardless of their culture. When my children were little, watching clouds together was a fun way to get them to stay still and hear what was on their minds. Even now that they are in their tween and teen stages, we enjoy looking at clouds on days like this, calling out to each other, "Oh look, can you see the horse?" or, "Yeah, and if you wait a minute it may have a chariot. See those clouds moving in behind it?" or, "I see a castle over there." Actually, those are comments typical of my daughters and me; my son will usually add something like, "Look! A frog with a Popsicle!" Sometimes we go on to form a narrative to tie the cloud pictures together.

This is a simple way of using our God-given imagination. I consider the irresistible urge to do so, and the joy such exercises give us, a unique stamp of being human, made in the image of God— the ultimate Creator and Storyteller. Of course, these flights of fantasy don't mean that my children and I don't know what clouds really are; in first grade, each of my children learned about the water cycle. Our power to see what the clouds might represent to us doesn't deny reality, it takes us higher. Our ability to find a cloud horse and chariot and have it carry us on to the telling of a story is one of the joys of being human and an indication that we are unique in all of creation.

On a more sophisticated level, reading and discussing fantasy, fairy tales, folklore, mythology, and legends holds similar enjoyment. Not only can we enjoy the story itself, we can go on to share what it means to us, what it reminds us of, and what that makes us think about in other stories and in real life. Such has been a treasured part of my family life. My husband and I have spent much time reading aloud with our children and discussing the stories we read. The outcome has been that we are raising avid readers and youngsters who can think both creatively and critically.

As Christians who take passing on our faith very seriously, our reading is always built on the foundation of the Bible as our standard of absolute truth; stories are discussed in relation to what the Bible teaches. However, we do not discourage reading fantasy just because it is fantasy, as long as we make sure our children have made the proper distinctions between fantasy and reality. We often use discussions that began with a fantasy story to lead into themes in the Bible, but our children are not confused into thinking that the Bible is to be treated as fantasy.

Then along came Harry Potter, and the Christian community became embroiled in heated debate between those asserting that the Harry Potter books were a veiled attempt to popularize occult practices, and those Christians (along with most of the rest of the world) who saw the stories as fantasy, following the age-old traditions of classic children's literature. I see how both sides can see it as they do, and I have tried to help both sides understand and be respectful of those with opposing convictions. This book is not meant to delve into that argument. (For more on this, see my previous book, *What's a Christian to Do with Harry Potter?* [Waterbrook Press, 2001].)

This book began as a counterpoint to one idea being put forward by anti-Potter critics, that just because they can look into the Harry Potter books in an attempt to find things they can correlate to real-world occult practices—and find some—that proves the Harry Potter books are about witchcraft. I disagree with that idea. This book is the friendliest way I could think of to ask people to stop and think about that again.

Let me give you an example. While publicly discussing my previous book, I encountered several people voicing beliefs along these lines: *I know all about the occult and real witchcraft. I went into Harry Potter looking to see if that is in these books and I found it.* One man counted sixty-four specific aspects of real-world witchcraft that correlate to something he found in Harry Potter. Since he was very familiar with real occult practices and knew far more about that than I know—or care to know—I take him at his word. I don't dispute what he saw there or the meaning it has come to carry for him.

However, it is the conclusion to such findings I want people to think about a little further. The conclusions are like this: *Since I have seen for myself that there are occult aspects to Harry Potter, I believe that Harry Potter popularizes, promotes, or perhaps intentionally hides real witchcraft and occult rituals. And I will not be dissuaded from this belief, regardless of what you show me to the contrary.* These conclusions take precedence over repeated denials by the author, because *they have seen it for themselves.*

To enter such an argument from this starting point usually results in hearing a laundry list of real occult practices that bear some resemblance to those referred to in Harry Potter, or more in-depth explanations of real-world witchcraft (which I am opposed to myself on biblical grounds, but don't care to be schooled in), or in simple name-calling. My response has been not to enter such arguments. Since the parties use different definitions, different forms of literary criticism, and different sources, the arguments are futile even when both parties believe the Bible. This book was prompted and shaped by this debate, although its content has far more to offer the reader.

My premise raises this question: What if I can use the same techniques of interpretation and selective reading, but look for the Christian gospel in the Harry Potter books? If I am able to find numerous parallels, would that prove that is what Harry Potter is about? (No.) Or might that reveal that the author has secretly hidden the gospel in her stories and is using witchcraft and wizardry as a disguise so unsuspecting children will not catch on? (No.) If, by using the same techniques, groups can find both the occult and Christian teachings in a fantasy story, what does that prove? I think it proves a point J. K. Rowling made.

When *Today* show host Katie Couric asked J. K. Rowling about accusations that she was using Harry Potter to lure children into Satanism, she flatly denied it. She said, "People tend to find in books what they look to find." That is my point. Some people go looking for the occult, and if they are well informed with regard to real-world witchcraft and occult rituals they may see that in the books. There are indeed points of similarity for readers who do not make a clear distinction between these fantasy stories and real life. They can then go on to fill that cloudy chariot with meaning and then to share that meaning with others. Indeed, they can point to specific parts of the books and say, "See!" and people can make out those shapes with their help. Such things are there to see and are worthy of discussion, but that does not mean that they are the only clouds in the sky.

Some may want to know my motivation. Given the divisive nature of this controversy, I have been misunderstood and denounced by all sides, Christians and non-Christians. Harry Potter fans assume that I am against Harry because I am a Christian, and Christian critics object to my using Harry Potter to spark spiritual discussions relating to the Bible. If you are not interested in this controversy, please skip ahead, but for those who care to know, here is a brief reply to the question *How could you?* Or for some, *Why bother?*

My most basic motivation is one I have held since January 31, 1973, when the story of God's love revealed in Jesus Christ suddenly became real to me. Since then, I have endeavored to communicate the Bible message in fresh ways so that those who have never really heard it can apprehend it. These motives are not ulterior. I ran across a mention of me and my previous book at the Wicca and Witchcraft News Web site. I was relieved to see that the article was titled, "Harry Potter Perverted to Preach Christ," and I took it as a backhanded compliment. I would have been troubled if they endorsed my Christian book. However, I took issue with their comment that I have "ulterior motives" in seeking to preach the gospel. Anyone who knows me knows that my life has been devoted to sharing the gospel, and I am not ashamed of that. So my motives are out in the open. The stunning story told in the Gospels has as much and more to offer than Harry's story, so I hope you will be open to hear it, perhaps for the first time.

The method of using something familiar to the culture to relate unfamiliar spiritual truth has been used by Christians back to the time of Christ, and by Jesus himself, even though it is guaranteed to cause raised eyebrows among some religious folks. Martin Luther did it when he used the familiar tunes of beer hall ballads to compose hymns. Jesus did it when he dared to make the hated Samaritan sinner the hero of one of his stories. The term "Good Samaritan" was an oxymoron to his audience. Therefore, I can confidently use this technique to communicate effectively with my culture too.

This technique is not something I devised when Harry Potter came along. I practiced this when I was a youth pastor and made a game of it with my own children. Once I had taught them the basic tenets from the Bible, I would have my kids (those in my youth group and later my own children) look at everything in our culture to see if they could find "glimmers of the gospel" by relating one to the other. Surprisingly, Harry Potter has more useful parallels to the gospel than almost any other piece of popular literature I have seen in decades.

I am alarmed that anti-Harry Potter sentiment has sparked book burnings by Christians. These have attracted media attention, and rightfully so, since the works being burned have expanded to include even Shakespeare, and many of those burning them have never read what they are burning. Even though this is an extreme and unusual occurrence, it has become almost the only mention of Christians with relation to Harry Potter. Almost no attention has been given to the many Christian leaders and educators who take a different view of Harry Potter, see both sides, enjoy, and/or recommend the Harry Potter books. I hope the media will use the discussion sparked by this book to counter some of the commotion and heightened emotion stirred up when they selectively report book burnings to the neglect of an alternative point of view that many Christians are trying to interject into this important public discourse.

Dubious distinctions are being made between the works of C. S. Lewis and J. R. R. Tolkien, as opposed to those of J. K. Rowling. The most basic is the suggestion that since Tolkien and Lewis were openly Christian and admitted that their faith worked its way into their fantasy—indeed, that it was an integral part—their fantasy is okay. However, since J. K. Rowling has been reserved in announcing her religious beliefs (although she openly declares her belief in God and attends the Church of Scotland), critics treat her fantasy as different in kind and inherently dangerous.

Do we really want to start determining what we will or will not read on the basis of whether the author shares our religious faith? If so, does it matter that Tolkien was a Catholic and Lewis was from the Anglican stream of Protestantism? Would those making such distinctions go on to read only that which is written by those of their own sect? Not only are Christians making such choices for themselves, some are seeking to ban such work in the public arena, thus threatening our cherished freedoms. Christians followed a similar path into the Dark Ages.

Is our own faith so fragile that we dare not know what those of a different sect of Christianity, or those of undisclosed religious persuasions, or those of different religious backgrounds are thinking? As a freedom-loving Christian and American, I hope and pray we never come to that. Perhaps this book can help us think this through again.

The kind of literary criticism being used by some Christians to discredit Harry Potter while touting Tolkien's and Lewis's fantasy writings is certainly not what Tolkien and Lewis taught their students. On this point I refer you to Thomas L. Martin, an expert far more knowledgeable than I. See his book *Reading the Classics with C. S. Lewis,* particularly the chapter "Lewis: A Critical Perspective." The essays on mythology and children's literature also touch on this subject.

★*★★*★*★*★*★*★*★*★*★*★*★*

In the epilogue to *Finding God in The Lord of the Rings,* Christian authors Kurt Bruner and Jim Ware say of Tolkien, "Fantasy, as he understood it, is, in its highest and purest form, a place where art, theology, and primal human desire meet and intersect." They conclude, "For the Christian this can mean only one thing: Fantasy is a place where we can come face to face with Christ."[1] I agree! So, to those who ask *How could you?* or *Why bother?* I answer: With all the uproar over Harry Potter in Christian circles, with all the wonderful parallels to the gospel waiting to be pointed out, with my desire to interest people who have been turned off by traditional ways of communicating the message, and with fantasy being a place where one may be able to "see Christ face to face," I could hardly resist.

I hope that you will enjoy thinking through the Harry Potter stories again and seeing new aspects of the story that may spark fresh thoughts and (hopefully) respectful discussions. Whatever our personal convictions or stance on the issues related to Harry Potter, I hope we can be guided by this biblical advice:

> But let everyone be quick to hear, slow to speak *and* slow to anger; for the anger of man does not achieve the righteousness of God. (Jas. 1:19b–20 NASB)

Notes to the Reader

1. This book is written primarily for those who have read the Harry Potter books already. My brief summary points are made for comparison to focus on the point at hand, not to give a literary overview of these books. If you have not read the books you can still enjoy the parallels, but I do not recommend substituting my summary, or anyone's, for the books themselves.

2. Since I am replicating the techniques used by anti-Potter critics to look for the opposite of what they were looking for, you can expect this work to be extremely selective. I admit that I went in with a metaphorical magnifying glass to look for "glimmers of the gospel" while at the same time I disregarded the other elements of the story that were not my focus of attention. I too object to this technique as a mode of serious literary criticism (what J. R. R. Tolkien and C. S. Lewis eschewed as reductionism). I am using it to cause readers to question how reliable such techniques are to literary criticism if the same can be used to "prove" two opposite conclusions.

3. I will be drawing parallels between the *fantasy* story told in the Harry Potter books and spiritual teachings and happenings in the Bible, declared to be true with regard to the *real world*. Since there are many similarities, we need to clearly distinguish between the fantasy world of Harry Potter and the real world.

4. For the sake of clarity, when paralleling spiritual insights and teachings of the Bible with elements of the Harry Potter stories, I will call the fantasy world in the Harry Potter books either "Harry's world" or "the wizarding world"; I will refer to the parallel (including supernatural aspects of our world revealed in the Bible) as "our

world" or "the real world," even though I do understand that some readers may not believe that the invisible realms and miraculous events described in the Bible are literally or factually real.

5. You do not have to be a Christian or even believe the Bible to enjoy drawing such parallels. I am hoping, however, that many will find their interest in the Bible sparked by looking at it in relation to things in the Harry Potter stories. For the record, I do believe the Bible to be God's word, a supernatural revelation from God to us. Even though it has happenings similar to some described in Harry's world, I do not read the Bible as fantasy. I believe our desire for the real (although veiled and miraculous) supernatural realm causes us to love fantasy stories that hint of worlds beyond our own. I view Harry's world as the fantasy sub-creation of J. K. Rowling, who uses "magic" as a literary device to tell a story. I view our world as it is revealed to be in the Bible. This includes accepting God's revelation about life in the material realm and spiritual realms that are invisible or only seen by those who have eyes to see. However, I hope that all readers—whether or not they hold the exact same view of Scripture that I do—will be able to find in this book glimpses of the gospel that will pique their interest and make them take another look at both the Harry Potter books and the Bible.

6. Given that I respect the author's stated intent and the work itself as a fantasy, I do not equate the "witchcraft" or "magic" of Harry's world with occult practices or witchcraft forbidden in the Bible, nor do I equate it with the Wiccan religion in our world. (If you want to understand how a Bible-believing Christian who rejects occult practices forbidden in the Bible can enjoy Harry Potter with a clean conscience, I refer you to my previous book, *What's a Christian to Do with Harry Potter?*)

7. Since I approach Harry Potter as fantasy, I will not stop to draw or refute any possible claims of a correlation between the literary "magic" of Harry's world with occult practices in our world. This book, in part, is a response to such claims and a counterpoint to that approach.

8. I laid out this book along the story lines of the four Harry Potter books published at the time of this writing. I did so to help

readers refresh their memories. I have been careful to keep each section focused on the book at hand, so as not to give away plot points in subsequent books. If you have not read all the books and do not want the plots revealed, only read the sections covering the books you have already read.

9. The page numbers in this book refer to the original hardcover editions of the Harry Potter books, published in North America by Arthur A. Levine/Scholastic and in the United Kingdom by Bloomsbury Children's Books.

Glimmers of the Gospel in Book One

Harry Potter and the Sorcerer's Stone

Introduction to Book One

I have had more opportunities than most to discuss Harry Potter with my fellow Christians. While conducting interviews for my previous book, *What's a Christian to Do with Harry Potter?* I found it disconcerting that more often than not the interviewer on a Christian radio broadcast had never read a Harry Potter book, but held views adamantly against the series. One host introduced me like this: "Next we'll be discussing the Harry Potter books. The first book, about to become a major motion picture, has this theme—and I quote—'There is no good or evil, only power and those too weak to seek it.' Our guest is a Christian who approves of the Harry Potter books. Mrs. Neal, please explain how you can support a book with such a theme."

I replied, "I'm afraid you're mistaken about that theme. The line you quoted is stated by one of the villains. The book clearly shows him to be evil and that believing the philosophy you quoted led to his downfall, indeed, to his death. The theme of the book is the opposite of what you concluded. It's a story about the necessity of resisting and defeating those who live by such a philosophy."

The host quickly asked another guest, opposed to Harry Potter but who had actually read the books, "Is what she said true?" He replied, "Well, . . . yes, but that's not really the point."

The host missed the theme of the story because she had been convinced it promoted evil. She had been shown only select items that related to occult practices so her concluding assumptions were upside down.

A magnifying glass does a fine job if you use it to examine something in detail. It is designed to exaggerate small areas and

3

magnify that small part for closer consideration. However, if you lift up a magnifying glass and try to view the entire room or landscape, the entire image flips upside down. This explains what happened above. As critics examine Harry Potter microscopically by looking specifically for any offending similarities to occult practices—or by listening to hearsay from those who have, as with this radio host—they run the risk of turning the theme of each book upside down. In literary terms, this approach is called reductionism. Such a practice of literary criticism was rejected by both C. S. Lewis and J. R. R. Tolkien. Reductionism was summed up nicely in the essay "Lewis: A Critical Perspective" in *Reading the Classics with C. S. Lewis*. There, Thomas L. Martin says this of those who practice reductionism: "Yet for their one slice of reality they should not think they have the whole pie."

I do not deny that those who have carefully examined the Harry Potter books to look specifically for elements that correlate to real world occult practices—which they are very familiar with—find some. However, I agree with Lewis and Tolkien's aversion to reductionism as a primary way of viewing literature—especially fantasy. I chose to use the reductionist approach myself in this book to show that such techniques could find the gospel as readily as the occult in Harry Potter.

There is a danger to this literary exercise I want to avoid. In taking up my literary magnifying glass to look for glimmers of the gospel in each book, I do not want to overlook the larger story and theme of the books in their entirety, nor do I want to give the impression that I believe the parts I magnify sum up the whole picture. To make sure my use of reductionism does not miss or misconstrue the real point, I have added a brief commentary on the general themes of each book in its entirety at the beginning of the section for that book. I hope these brief interludes between books will let you put down the magnifying glass I have raised for the purpose of one kind of instruction, so that you may think more broadly about the worthy themes the Harry Potter stories raise for us.

Even in considering the broader themes of each story, I look at these from a Judeo-Christian perspective. Perhaps of great surprise to many who have heard only negative things against Harry Potter, I believe that the general themes of each book uphold and promote foundational beliefs and Judeo-Christian values emphasized throughout the Bible. I had considered including specific Bible verses but found that the themes were so pervasive throughout the Bible that that would not be necessary. Even those not well versed in the Bible will be able to recognize that these themes are indeed biblical.

The major themes of Book One are the triumph of good over evil and the power of love. We meet a boy who enters a realm where the villain and his servant are seeking immortality so that the evil villain can seize power and rule over those who hold firmly to that which is good. The villain's philosophy, adopted by his servant, is "there is no good or evil, only power and those too weak to seek it." In order to thwart the destructive aims of the villain, Harry and his friends must understand that there is a fundamental difference between good and evil, and that to let evil prevail is to accept murderous and destructive oppression in their world. To resist evil and keep evil from overpowering good, Harry and his friends must do their part, alongside the adults.

Throughout the story, courage and self-sacrifice are required to overcome evil with good. The greatest example of this is how Harry's mother sacrifices herself to protect her baby, thus causing the curse of death to rebound on the evil villain. That destroyed his power partially, but the story shows that unless evil is destroyed utterly, it will always seek to regain power. Therefore, those on the side of good must persist in their resistance to the forces of evil.

The Curse of Death
and the Boy Who Lived

*"That's what yeh get when a powerful, evil curse touches
yeh—took care of yer mum an' dad an' yer house, even—
but it didn't work on you, an' that's why yer famous, Harry.
No one ever lived after he decided ter kill 'em, no one
except you."*

—Hagrid to Harry, Book One, p. 55

*B*efore Harry was born, a wizard "went . . . bad. As bad as you could go. Worse. Worse than worse." He terrorized the wizarding world with a deadly curse. The Dark Lord Voldemort murdered Harry's father, then threw the curse of death at Harry, but Harry's mother loved him so much that she threw herself in front of the curse to shield him. With Harry's parents both dead, baby Harry seemed helpless. Voldemort hit him with the curse again. But, instead of killing Harry, the curse rebounded on Voldemort. His power was mysteriously broken. He disappeared, and his reign of terror came to an abrupt end.

This "great myst'ry"—as Hagrid calls it—is the mystery of love. Lily Potter loved her son so much that she laid down her life for his. Hagrid said there was something going on that night that Voldemort had not counted on. Something about Harry stumped him, and Harry became famous as "the boy who lived."

This is where the story begins, with the whole wizarding world rejoicing, sending owls and shooting stars across the sky in an unrestrained outburst of joy. Their celebration was so great, it was even sighted in the Muggle world. Showers of shooting stars all over Britain, indeed! Owls flying in daylight!

The Bible says that before the world began, an angel went bad. Worse. Worse than worse. He rebelled, turning from light to darkness. God cast him out of heaven, and he began looking for ways to bring death and destruction on the people God had made in his image. This fallen angel lured the first man and woman to disobey God. When they did, they were hit with a deadly curse—which God had warned them against. From that time on the whole world lived in fear of the curse of death.

The love Lily Potter demonstrated for her infant son—to the point of being willing to lay down her life for him—can remind us of the love of Jesus Christ: "For while we were still helpless, at the right time Christ died for the ungodly. For one will hardly die for a righteous man; though perhaps for the good man someone would dare even to die. But God demonstrates His own love toward us, in that while we were yet sinners, Christ died for us" (Rom. 5:6–8 NASB).

Apparently this was not something the evil one in our world had counted on either. The curse of death was broken and rebounded in life, not only for Jesus but for everyone who believes in him: "For God so loved the world that he gave his only Son, so that everyone who believes in him may not perish but may have eternal life" (John 3:16).

The opening scene of Harry Potter's story is reminiscent of another story we all know, when a baby slept out in the cold night air while the residents of another realm broke through the skies to proclaim their unrestrained joy to the world.

A Lightning Bolt Scar

*Under a tuft of jet-black hair over his forehead they could
see a curiously shaped cut, like a bolt of lightning.*
—Book One, p. 15

*T*he Dark Lord wielded such destructive power that most people in the wizarding world were afraid even to speak his name. Instead, they called him "He-Who-Must-Not-Be-Named" or "You-Know-Who." He killed without remorse, inflicted torturous pain on his victims, and made them do whatever he decreed, usually to their own harm. No wonder people were terrified of him. No wonder those who were not followers of the Dark Lord celebrated when he was brought down.

The Bible reveals that "the evil one" in our world has control over fallen angels, also known as demons. These evil spirits at times torment, even take control of people, forcing them to do terrible things against their will and to their own harm. The force of evil can also be seen when oppressive regimes hold control over nations. Evil is real, it is loose in the world, and the Bible tells us that "the Son of God was revealed for this purpose, to destroy the works of the devil" (1 John 3:8).

Throughout the accounts given in the four Gospels, we see that whenever Jesus came into an area, people would bring to him those who were possessed by or under the influence of demons. Jesus commanded these spirits to leave the people they afflicted. At his

8

word, these evil spirits had to go. When this happened, some people who had been paralyzed could walk, some who had been deaf could hear, some who had been unable to speak could speak again, some who were suffering from lingering illnesses were freed from the bondage of their diseases.

At one point, Jesus gave seventy of his disciples the power to cast out demons in his name. They were sent out to preach about the kingdom of God. As they preached, they validated their claims that the kingdom of God was more powerful than the kingdom of darkness by casting out demons. Even the disciples were amazed that the demons were subject to them in Jesus' name. Jesus told them, "I watched Satan fall from heaven like a flash of lightning. See, I have given you authority to tread on snakes and scorpions, and over all the power of the enemy; and nothing will hurt you" (Luke 10:18–19). Because God was more powerful than Satan, God cast him out *like lightning.*

So the lightning bolt scar on Harry's forehead can serve as a reminder that the curse of death was broken (which is what happened when Harry got his scar) and that good is more powerful than evil. Jesus gave his disciples the power to "trample on snakes and scorpions"—demonic influences—"and to overcome all the power of the enemy" (Luke 10:19 NIV). Therefore, although they are real and dangerous, we need not cower in fear of evil spirits. Like Harry and friends, we can learn to practice Defense Against the Dark Arts, trusting that there is a greater power at work that we may not yet fully understand.

Scars Can Come in Handy

"Is that where—?" whispered Professor McGonagall.
"Yes," said Dumbledore. "He'll have that scar forever."
"Couldn't you do something about it, Dumbledore?"
"Even if I could, I wouldn't. Scars can come in handy."
—Book One, p. 15

*H*arry was hit with the death curse by the evil Lord Voldemort. The cut was still fresh when Hagrid, Dumbledore, and Professor McGonagall first saw it. He had been hit, yet, astonishingly, he was alive! That cut would become a famous scar, standing silent witness to the facts of history in Harry's life and the wizarding world. As Dumbledore pointed out, "Scars can come in handy," like the one on his knee that is a perfect map of the London Underground. Harry's scar would remind all who saw it that there is something more powerful than the curse of death.

The Christian gospel makes the startling assertion that God entered history by becoming incarnate in human flesh. With that, "Myth became fact," as C. S. Lewis put it.[2] God became a baby, who grew up to lay down his life as a sacrifice for us. That is how he received the wounds and cuts as the curse of death hit him. He was nailed to a cross, hands and feet, before many witnesses. To prove he was truly dead, the Roman executioner pierced his side with a spear. The flow of blood and water proved his heart had ruptured and that he was verifiably dead. His enemies feared his disciples would

10

steal the body and then say he had risen from the dead. So, at their request, his tomb was guarded by soldiers. A crucified man, rising from the dead! Who would believe such a story? But they dared not leave that to chance.

On the third day after the crucifixion, wild stories began to circulate. Most of Jesus' closest disciples were convinced, except for Thomas. He was far too logical to accept such emotionally charged rumors as truth. He said to the other disciples, "Unless I see the mark of the nails in his hands, and put my finger in the mark of the nails and my hand in his side, I will not believe" (John 20:25).

That would be arranged. A week later, Jesus' disciples were all together, and Thomas was with them:

> Although the doors were shut, Jesus came and stood among them and said, "Peace be with you." Then he said to Thomas, "Put your finger here and see my hands. Reach out your hand and put it in my side. Do not doubt but believe." Thomas answered him, "My Lord and my God!" Jesus said to him, "Have you believed because you have seen me? Blessed are those who have not seen and yet have come to believe." (John 20:26–29)

The wounds were still fresh for Thomas; the rest of us will have to make do with scars.

I dare say those scars will be as famous in our world as Harry's scar is in the wizarding world. The Bible predicts a day when those scars will be seen by all—those who believe and those who remain in doubt: "Look! He is coming with the clouds; every eye will see him, even those who pierced him" (Rev. 1:7). People stare at Harry's scar when they see it for themselves for the first time. Before, it had just been something they had read or heard about. What a day that will be when everyone sees the scars Jesus bears and comes to realize that the stories they heard were true accounts of something remarkable that actually happened, leaving a lasting reminder in the form of a scar etched in human flesh.

The Unstoppable Invitation

*Uncle Vernon stayed at home again. After burning all the
letters, he got out a hammer and nails and boarded up the
cracks around the front and back doors.*
                                            —Book One, p. 40

*P*oor Harry! Never in all his life had he received a letter addressed
personally to him. So when a letter arrived for him, he was amazed.
Whoever sent it treated him with respect, addressing him as "Mr.
H. Potter." Someone out there knew where he lived, but beyond
that, knew that his "bedroom" was the cupboard under the stairs.

Who wouldn't be eager for Harry to open such a letter? The
answer is Uncle Vernon. He made it his highest priority to keep
Harry from receiving his letter, despite Harry's best efforts to lay
hold of one. I say one, because the first—and many subsequent—
letters were intercepted and destroyed by Uncle Vernon. When he
found it impossible to stop the letters from arriving at 4 Privet
Drive, Uncle Vernon made a mad dash to escape. But every time,
whoever was sending the letters knew precisely where to find
Harry. This had to be maddening to Uncle Vernon, but comforting
to Harry. When Harry finally received his hand-delivered invitation, it was addressed as follows:

> Mr. H. Potter
> The Floor
> Hut-on-the-Rock
> The Sea

God would not be deterred in getting his invitation delivered to humanity. Even though some people act like Uncle Vernon and try to escape, there is no way to successfully run away from God, who is by nature omniscient and omnipresent. King David recorded these truths in one of his psalms:

> O LORD, you have searched me
>   and you know me.
> You know when I sit and when I rise;
>   you perceive my thoughts from afar.
> You discern my going out and my lying down;
>   you are familiar with all my ways.
> Before a word is on my tongue
>   you know it completely, O LORD.
> You hem me in—behind and before;
>   you have laid your hand upon me.
> Such knowledge is too wonderful for me,
>   too lofty for me to attain.
> Where can I go from your Spirit?
>   Where can I flee from your presence?
> If I go up to the heavens, you are there;
>   if I make my bed in the depths, you are there.
> If I rise on the wings of the dawn,
>   if I settle on the far side of the sea,
> even there your hand will guide me,
>   your right hand will hold me fast.
>   (Psalm 139:1–10 NIV)

There is Someone out there who knows each of us, loves us, cares about our situation, and calls us each by name. His message has been sent out through prophets who wrote it down, read it aloud, and delivered it to kings and peasants, religious and irreligious, young and old alike. God's message, compiled in the Bible, holds an invitation to enter a supernatural realm where we can learn his ways and take an active part in the battle between good and evil.

God's message has also encountered great opposition and inter-ference, at times quite similar to Uncle Vernon's burning Harry's letters. Once God sent a particularly unwelcome message through his prophet Jeremiah to a king who did not want anyone to receive the message. In those days, the message was dictated to a scribe who painstakingly wrote it by hand on a scroll. As the scroll with Jeremiah's prophecy was read to the king, he cut it off, piece by piece, and burned it in the fire. He assumed that would be the end of that. But the message could not be deterred. God repeated the message to Jeremiah, who delivered it to the king again, with a few choice words added to it (see Jer. 36:23–32).

As it became necessary to have Harry's letter delivered in per-son, a time likewise came for God to send his message in person: "In the beginning was the Word, and the Word was with God, and the Word was God. He was in the beginning with God" (John 1:1). "The Word became flesh and lived among us, and we have seen his glory, the glory as of a father's only son, full of grace and truth" (John 1:14).

Jesus came on a mission to seek out and save those who are lost. Harry may have thought he was lost out on that rock in the middle of the sea, but he was not lost to Hagrid. Hagrid would not stop until he had fulfilled the mission given him by Dumbledore to deliver Harry's invitation to attend Hogwarts. Likewise, God's Holy Spirit continues to seek out those who are lost and to urge them to accept God's invitation to come into his kingdom and learn of him.

The Leaky Cauldron:
A Door to an Unseen World

*The people hurrying by didn't glance at it. Their eyes slid
from the big book shop on one side to the record shop on
the other as if they couldn't see the Leaky Cauldron at all.
In fact, Harry had the most peculiar feeling that only he
and Hagrid could see it.*

—Book One, p. 68

*H*agrid and Harry took the train to London on their way to buy
Harry's school supplies. Harry was a bit astonished that one could
buy such things in London. According to Hagrid, you just had to
know where to go. Hagrid led Harry to the Leaky Cauldron, but it
seemed to Harry that the people passing by did not even see the
entrance. It proved real enough—a doorway from our world into
the magical one for those who could see it and knew which bricks
to tap to get into Diagon Alley.

Spiritual things are funny that way. Some people have eyes to see
them and others don't. It seems that prophets and children are more
likely than others to be able to see what some cannot. There is an
account in the Bible when Elisha the prophet of Israel was not only
able to see what others could not see, but hear what others could
not hear—such as what the king was saying in private. So the king
sent his armies to arrest the prophet. Elisha was not worried, but
his servant was quite upset at seeing a sizable force coming for
them. Elisha urged calm: "'Do not be afraid, for there are more

15

with us than there are with them.' Then Elisha prayed: 'O LORD, please open his eyes that he may see.' So the LORD opened the eyes of the servant, and he saw; the mountain was full of horses and chariots of fire all around Elisha" (2 Kgs. 6:15–17).

The state of someone's heart can affect his or her ability to see things in the spiritual realm. Jesus told his disciples that the reason he taught people in parables was because the lessons were for some to see and others not to see. He explained by relating this to a prophecy by Isaiah that states, "For this people's heart has become calloused; they hardly hear with their ears, and they have closed their eyes. Otherwise they might see with their eyes, hear with their ears, understand with their hearts and turn, and I would heal them" (Matt. 13:15 NIV).

Those who "have eyes to see" such things are counted as blessed, but there is an element of revelation that must take place. Even Jesus' own disciples seemed to be unable to see what Jesus was getting at or to recognize the way into the kingdom they were seeking. (And this was after three years of following him.) Shortly before Jesus' departure back to heaven, he consoled his disciples:

> "Do not let your hearts be troubled. Believe in God, believe also in me. In my Father's house there are many dwelling places. If it were not so, would I have told you that I go to prepare a place for you? And if I go and prepare a place for you, I will come again and will take you to myself, so that where I am, there you may be also. And you know the way to the place where I am going." Thomas said to him, "Lord, we do not know where you are going. How can we know the way?" Jesus said to him, "I am the way, and the truth, and the life. No one comes to the Father except through me." (John 14:1–6)

The crowds that hurry by the Leaky Cauldron without seeing that doorway into another realm can remind us that many have eyes but do not see either the supernatural battles taking place around them or the doorway into the kingdom of God. Those things are invisible to them, or perhaps are just a blur among all the other attractions of the world.

Diagon Alley: First Stop, Gringotts

"D'yeh think yer parents didn't leave yeh anything?"
—Hagrid to Harry, Book One, p. 63

*B*efore setting out for Hogwarts, Hagrid took Harry to Diagon Alley to get his school supplies. Harry was concerned that he would not be able to get what he needed because the Dursleys had never given him spending money. Harry soon learned that his parents had set aside a small fortune for him, kept safely in the vault at Gringotts, the wizards' bank. Of course, the currency of the wizarding world is different from that in the world where Harry had grown up, but it would get him everything he needed in the wizarding world.

Similarly, there are riches available to us in the kingdom of God that are not recognized in the world in which we live. Harry arrived at Gringotts technically poor, but left with enough to buy goodies from the cart to share with Ron; so too Paul was able to rightly describe himself and his fellow servants of God as "poor, yet making many rich; as having nothing, and yet possessing everything" (2 Cor. 6:10). The Bible promises that "God will meet all your needs according to his glorious riches in Christ Jesus" (Phil. 4:19 NIV). This covers a simple assurance that our basic physical and material needs will be met but also includes "the full riches of complete understanding, in order that they may know the mystery of God, namely, Christ, in whom are hidden all the treasures of wisdom and knowledge" (Col. 2:2).

The riches set aside for Harry by his loving parents will give him everything he needs for life and for his education at Hogwarts so he can grow to be completely equipped to operate well in the magical world, particularly by defending against the Dark Arts. Likewise, God's "divine power has given us everything we need for life and godliness through our knowledge of him who called us by his own glory and goodness. Through these he has given us his very great and precious promises, so that through them you may participate in the divine nature and escape the corruption in the world caused by evil desires" (2 Pet. 1:3–5 NIV).

Having previously known financial deprivation and the shame that comes with it, Harry is sensitive to those who have less than he. So, too, Christians are commanded to be sensitive to those who are poor in this world's goods, to not look down on those who have less but, rather, to treat them with respect (see Jas. 2:5).

Getting onto Platform Nine and Three-Quarters

"All you have to do is walk straight at the barrier between platforms nine and ten. . . . Best do it at a bit of a run if you're nervous."
—Mrs. Weasley to Harry, Book One, p. 93

After receiving his invitation to Hogwarts, Harry still had to get there. Hagrid had given him a ticket for the Hogwarts Express, but Harry had to get onto the right platform. Uncle Vernon laughed derisively when he left Harry at King's Cross Station standing between platforms nine and ten, with his trunk and Hedwig's cage. There had to be a way to get onto platform nine and three-quarters, but Harry didn't know how until the Weasleys showed up. It did seem a bit odd—just walk straight into the barrier.

The process for getting onto platform nine and three-quarters was something anyone *could* do, but no reasonable person *would* do unless he or she believed that was the way—however strange it might seem to onlookers—to find the platform. Harry watched the Weasleys go through, one by one. Mrs. Weasley offered her encouragement, and Harry followed her instructions. He reached the platform and was able to see the Hogwarts Express and experience what others could not. He came out onto platform nine and three quarters the same person, but he had stepped into a whole new world of possibilities and was now on his way to learning how to function in the supernatural world.

19

The Uncle Vernons of the world say, "Seeing is believing." Faith says, "Believing is seeing." Or as the Letter to the Hebrews puts it, "Now faith is the assurance of things hoped for, the conviction of things not seen" (Heb. 11:1). Therefore, *if* you believe, you are willing to act on what you believe, which is why real faith leads to decisive actions. There is also merit to being guided by those who have already entered the spiritual realm. Mrs. Weasley's advice is reminiscent of the Nike slogan, "Just do it!" In athletic and spiritual terms, the way to begin moving toward power, greater prowess, and victory is to "just do it." But do what? What is the spiritual act called for in order to enter the invisible kingdom of God?

Strange as it might seem to onlookers, the point of entry given in the Bible is baptism. John the Baptist came to prepare the way for the Lord. He told people to come down to the Jordan River, repent of their sins, go under the water, then come up to a new life. Even though Jesus was born without sin, he came to John and asked to be baptized "to fulfill all righteousness" (Matt. 3:15). He led so his followers would see the prescribed way to enter the kingdom of God. When Jesus came up out of the water, we know it "worked" because of what happened—even the "Muggles" of his day could see. Matthew describes it this way: "And when Jesus had been baptized, just as he came up from the water, suddenly the heavens were opened to him and he saw the Spirit of God descending like a dove and alighting on him. And a voice from heaven said, 'This is my Son, the Beloved, with whom I am well pleased'" (Matt. 3:16–17).

Jesus invited everyone to come, even common people. Many of them obeyed the instructions of John the Baptist and Jesus by getting baptized. However, many of the religious leaders scoffed and refused; therefore, they did not get into the kingdom of God (see Luke 7:30). Here is the ticket we have been handed: "The one who believes and is baptized will be saved; but the one who does not believe will be condemned" (Mark 16:16).

Later, after the disciples received power from heaven, Peter addressed a crowd. They wanted to know how to get in. He said, "Repent, and be baptized every one of you in the name of Jesus

Christ so that your sins may be forgiven; and you will receive the gift of the Holy Spirit. For the promise is for you, for your children, and for all who are far away, everyone whom the Lord our God calls to him" (Acts 2:38). Here we see the connection between obeying the instructions in this natural world and entering into a realm where supernatural power becomes suddenly available.

Just as Harry believed in what he could not see, and was prompted to obey even odd-sounding instructions, likewise those who believe God's word will obey it and will follow the path of those who went before us into God's kingdom.

The Sorting

Harry gripped the edges of the stool and thought, Not
Slytherin, not Slytherin.
*"Not Slytherin, eh?" said the small voice. "Are you sure?
. . . Well, if you're sure—better be GRYFFINDOR!"*
—Book One, p. 121

*E*ven before Harry arrived at Hogwarts he began to wonder where
he would fit in. He had met Draco Malfoy while getting his robes
fitted and heard more than he cared to about Malfoy's preference
for Slytherin House. He met the Weasleys and recognized how different they were from Malfoy, and they were all in Gryffindor. His
parents had been in Gryffindor too. (Hufflepuffs were just, loyal,
true, and hard working. Ravenclaws were known for their wit,
learning, and ready mind.) Then there was that important bit of history: Every wizard known to have gone over to the evil side had
been in Slytherin.

Harry and the other first years were worried that they would
have to pass some kind of test or wrestle a troll to get to be chosen. Harry even worried that he might not be chosen at all. But
soon the sorting was underway and they were all sorted into the
houses that would become like their family while at Hogwarts.
With Harry's turn we learn a bit more of what goes on under the
hat. Harry thought, *"Not Slytherin!"* and that came into play as the
hat decided where to place him. Once the hat shouted out
"GRYFFINDOR!" Harry was relieved just to have been chosen
and not put in Slytherin.

The mystery of the sorting ceremony brings up some interesting thoughts. Harry resisted evil, and was sorted into Gryffindor. He was "chosen" to be a Gryffindor, but also exercised free will. He wanted to follow in his parents' footsteps, and did not yield to the hat's suggestion that he could be great in Slytherin. Perhaps the hat was only testing him. Perhaps he was destined for Gryffindor all along, chosen before he ever sat on the stool, but the hat wanted to give him the chance to exercise his own will by choosing to resist evil.

This parallels one of the paradoxes of Christianity that theologians have debated for centuries. We are "chosen" by God's grace, but we are also created with free will, so our allegiance to God and opposition to evil will not be robotic. There is an interplay between predestination, alluded to in Ephesians 4:1 (NASB), "He chose us in Him before the foundation of the world," and free will, as in "And let everyone who hears say, 'Come.' And let everyone who is thirsty come. Let anyone who wishes take the water of life as a gift" (Rev. 22:17). This interplay holds a perplexing mystery.

We see the same kind of perplexity at Harry's sorting. There is a growing sense throughout the books that Harry is predestined to some great calling, and yet we see him going through the process of *choosing* to resist evil and *being chosen* to go into the house of the lion, Gryffindor House. It was founded by Godric Gryffindor, and includes a long line of those who have bravely fought evil, James and Lily Potter among them. In biblical terms, Jesus is referred to as the "Lion of the tribe of Judah" (Rev. 5:5), acknowledging his human ancestry from Judah, one of the twelve sons of Israel. Revelation shows Jesus pitted against "that ancient serpent, who is called the Devil and Satan, the deceiver of the whole world—he was thrown down to the earth, and his angels were thrown down with him" (Rev. 12:9). This reminds us of Slytherins, whose symbol is the serpent and whose nature reveals a cunning and willingness to use any means to achieve their ends. The cunning and deceptive nature of the serpent was witnessed in the temptation of Adam and Eve in the garden and is referred to in the New Testament (see 2 Cor. 11:3).

So the basic imagery of the rivalry and conflict between Gryffindor and Slytherin parallels the basic imagery of the Bible's description of the battle between those on God's side and Satan. But please note: It is important to remember that the Harry Potter stories are fantasy, and *never mention Satan*. Any parallels in that regard are drawn in the mind of the reader by making a correlation between the wizarding world of Harry Potter and the supernatural world the Bible reveals in the real world.

Dumbledore's Dire Warning

*"I must tell you that this year, the third-floor corridor on
the right-hand side is out of bounds to everyone who does
not wish to die a very painful death."*
——Dumbledore to students, Book One, p. 127

*H*arry didn't quite know what to make of Dumbledore's dire
warning, given at the start-of-school banquet his first year. At first
he thought the headmaster couldn't be serious, but Percy put that
idea to rest. What kind of headmaster makes such a pronouncement to students? Was he joking? Apparently not. Was he being
cruel? Not Dumbledore. From the start, his kindness, care for the
students, calmness, and good humor were apparent. So how does
this make sense?

Dumbledore was simply telling the truth. He knew that there
was a real danger in that corridor. Fluffy, the three-headed dog,
could indeed cause a very painful death to any students who went
where they were warned not to go. Dumbledore, as headmaster,
knew things the students were not supposed to know. He was under
no obligation to explain himself to them—not even to the prefects,
to Percy's chagrin.

Some who did not understand what was going on behind the
scenes might think Dumbledore was being mean. *How could he
scare them so? They're only children.* But he was not being mean.
On the contrary, his dire warning was meant to spare them pain.
Granted, Harry, Ron, Neville, and Hermione did not heed his warning closely enough and got the scare of their lives. Once they realized what was in that corridor and why, Dumbledore's warning

made sense. It also reinforced their growing understanding that Dumbledore was a refuge for them, one who would do everything in his power—which was considerable—to keep them safe.

In the opening pages of the Bible, at the very beginning of the relationship between God and humanity, God gives a dire warning: "You are free to eat from any tree in the garden; but you must not eat from the tree of the knowledge of good and evil, for when you eat of it you will surely die" (Gen. 2:16–17). Was God just trying to scare the man? Was God being cruel? No. God simply understood what would happen if anyone ate from that particular tree. It was because God did not want people to experience death that he gave that warning.

We know that the man and woman in the garden of Eden did not heed the warning. They paid far more heavily than Harry and company. When they disobeyed, precisely what God warned would happen did happen. Death came into their lives. They did not die on the spot, but they began to die. Those whom God intended to live eternally without death and corruption became corrupt. They immediately fell under the penalty of death spiritually (separated from God with a disposition toward sin) and subject to mortality and physical death. Eventually, one of the sons of Adam and Eve killed his brother, and they experienced a kind of death in their own souls too (see Gen. 3 and 4).

God's warnings simply tell us what he knows to be true so that we can avoid the pain, danger, and death he wants to spare us. When God warns us away from sin, it is because he knows therein lies danger. When God warns of hell, he is not being cruel. He is not trying to scare us unnecessarily. Hell is scary, but since God knows that hell is a terrible reality, he would be cruel not to warn us. The older students who knew Dumbledore well trusted that he was serious in his warning but also kind. Likewise, those who have been close to God for a while will be the first to tell others that God's warnings are to be taken seriously, but that they are in keeping with his nature, which is love.

Hagrid's Temptation

"Hagrid's always wanted a dragon, he told me so the first
   time I ever met him," said Harry.
"But it's against our laws," said Ron.

—Book One, p. 230

*H*agrid has a fondness for dangerous magical creatures, even illegal ones like dragons. As a boy, he even tried raising werewolf
cubs. So when the opportunity arose to have a dragon's egg, how
could Hagrid refuse? He was at a pub down in the village when a
friendly stranger struck up a conversation, bought him a few
drinks—another of Hagrid's weaknesses—and showed Hagrid a
dragon's egg. He suggested playing cards for it. It never dawned
on Hagrid that there might be more at stake than an egg.

Hagrid knew it was wrong to keep the dragon; that is why he
pulled his curtains closed. But Harry, Ron, and Hermione were
much more concerned about the illegality of having the egg than
Hagrid. He was too taken with his lifelong desire to have a dragon.
Hagrid lovingly stoked the fire to keep the egg hot, waiting with
anticipation for it to hatch. From the moment it hatched, the baby
dragon was sneezing sparks and snapping at Hagrid's fingers, but
Hagrid was as protective of his pet as if it were his child.

The increasing dangers were apparent to Hagrid's friends. Norbert the dragon grew at an alarming rate, which made hiding the
dragon more of a challenge. Malfoy had caught sight of it and could
report Hagrid to the authorities. Hagrid became derelict in his
duties because Norbert demanded so much of his time and attention: feeding him, hiding him, keeping others from discovering his

secret. Besides, as Hermione pointed out, dragons breathe fire and Hagrid lives in a wooden house!

Hagrid kept making excuses for Norbert. Even when the dragon bit Ron with its poisonous fangs, Hagrid told Ron off and went on singing "baby Norbert" a lullaby. Even when Norbert took to biting Hagrid's leg, Hagrid passed it off as "jus' playin'." Eventually, Hermione, Harry, and Ron helped Hagrid realize that he simply could not manage the situation. They convinced him to let them send Norbert off to Charlie Weasley, who was legally studying wild dragons in Romania.

This is a striking image of the process by which one is tempted and progresses into a life dominated by sin. The Bible teaches that whenever we are tempted, "no one should say, 'God is tempting me.' For God cannot be tempted by evil, nor does he tempt anyone; but each one is tempted when, by his own evil desire, he is dragged away and enticed" (Jas. 1:13–14 NIV).

Just as there was a personality behind the temptation Hagrid experienced, one with ulterior motives, so too behind all sin there is an evil one who generally is up to no good. However, we are tempted by those things each one of us desires. Hagrid just happened to have a hankering for a dragon. Each person is attracted to some things that are against God's law, but these differ according to the person. When the opportunity arises for us to have what we have always wanted or fantasized about having—even though we know it is wrong—and we are enticed by our own desire, that is where temptation begins.

The progress from temptation to sin to the consequences goes like this: After desire has conceived, it gives birth to sin; sin, when it is full grown, gives birth to death (see Jas. 1:15). Just as it is the nature of the dragon to grow up to breathe fire and use its poisonous fangs, so it is the nature of sin to progress to deadly proportions. Sometimes this means death to good relationships or self-respect; sometimes it means death to the one who is caught up in a delusion over sin, or in trying to cover up the shame of it.

When people become protective of their sins, the first thing that happens is that they close the curtains of their lives, hiding in shame and trying to keep out the prying eyes of those who might force them to give up what they know is wrong but dearly want to keep. From the very first sin, we see this to be true. Adam and Eve were *hiding* in the garden after they disobeyed God. To this day, the desire to conceal that which we know is wrong is a hallmark of living with sin. Jesus described it this way: "For all who do evil hate the light and do not come to the light, so that their deeds may not be exposed" (John 3:20).

When someone is caught up in sin—even a nice person—that person needs friends who will confront the problem and help get rid of the sin. This is not to be done in a condemning way, but gently, since all of us are prone to temptation and sin. These are the instructions found in the Letter to the Galatians: "If someone is caught in a sin, you who are spiritual should restore him gently. But watch yourself, or you also may be tempted. Carry each other's burdens, and in this way you will fulfill the law of Christ" (Gal. 6:1–3 NIV). At the heart of the gospel is the promise that there is a way we can get rid of our guilt for sin (in general), but it goes on to show us how to help each other get rid of particular sins that threaten our own well-being as well as the lives of others.

Hagrid's temptation gives us a good model of the destructive, dangerous, and potentially deadly consequences of giving in to our sinful desires. Harry, Ron, and Hermione model a biblical way of helping someone caught up in the delusions and dangers of sin. We see this in their concern, the way they spoke the truth in love and eventually carried their friend's burden—this time in the shape of a Norwegian Ridgeback dragon—up to the tower to be taken away so Hagrid could be free of it.

Note: Some may be troubled that Harry and Hermione broke school rules in getting rid of Norbert. For those attuned to such details, it might be noted that they were willing to break a lesser rule to accomplish the greater good of protecting the whole school from a dangerous dragon. However, they did risk punishment to do so, were caught, and willingly accepted their punishment as fitting because they did break a rule.

Dangerous Designs of the Dragon-Egg Dealer

"Don't you think it's a bit odd," said Harry, . . . "that what Hagrid wants more than anything else is a dragon, and a stranger turns up who just happens to have an egg in his pocket?"
—Harry to Ron and Hermione, Book One, p. 265

*T*he stranger Hagrid met in the pub was not simply looking for a friendly game of cards. He came in with the intention of getting Hagrid drunk and seeing if he could find out how to get past Fluffy, the three-headed dog Dumbledore had borrowed to help guard the Sorcerer's Stone. After a few drinks, Hagrid volunteered that he had always really wanted a dragon. Funny, that's just what the hooded stranger managed to pull out of his pocket. But before he would let Hagrid have the dragon's egg, Hagrid would have to convince him that he could handle it. What experience did he have with other dangerous magical creatures? Indeed, the hooded stranger seemed very interested in Fluffy.

Hagrid hadn't given the stranger's intentions much thought. That was a mistake. It took Harry a while, but eventually it dawned on Harry that it was strange that Hagrid was offered what he had always wanted but the stranger sought nothing in return—or did he? Indeed, he got what he was scheming to get all along: the secret of how to get past Fluffy.

But that was not the extent of the scheming that went on under that hood! Later, when Professor Quirrell revealed that he was the one hiding under that cloak, we learned that his real aim was to steal the Sorcerer's Stone, kill Harry, and give the stone to his master, Lord Voldemort. That would give Voldemort the wealth and immortality he sought so that he could regain power and dominate the wizarding world again. Would Hagrid have ever thought a game of cards with a stranger—albeit one who held the fulfillment to an illicit desire in his pocket—could contribute to the destruction of Hogwarts or lead to Harry's death? Perhaps, but only in retrospect. Unfortunately, Hagrid was outwitted by the deceptive schemes of one working on the side of evil.

What appeared to be a chance encounter was later revealed to be much more. There was an intelligent force working toward evil aims hiding under a cloak of secrecy. When the Bible warns against "the evil one" or Satan, it does not describe a general force of evil, but rather an evil personality with evil intentions. We are warned to be aware of his schemes, alert to the danger of being outwitted, and that we should not be "ignorant of his designs" (2 Cor. 2:11; see also Eph. 6:11). The word *schemes* denotes a pattern of thought, a plan that is in keeping with the nature and intentions of the one doing the planning.

Therefore, if we know the overall intentions of those on the side of evil—both people and the spiritual forces of evil motivating them—we can think more critically when we face decisions. This understanding of the nature of the evil one (hateful, deceptive, and murderous) along with a general understanding of his aims (coming to steal, kill, and destroy) can inform us so that we are not outwitted.

The upside of this understanding of our struggle against evil is that we can learn to make more intelligent decisions to fend off dangerous deceptions. We must stop and back up a little whenever we are in a situation where sin is handed to us.

I cannot help but think of publicly disgraced ministers who must not have been thinking straight when they gave in to temptations to engage in sexual sin or to mishandle funds or power. Surely they should have anticipated that "the evil one" was working behind the scenes with dangerous designs to discredit and destroy their reputation, family, and ministry. Surely, if they had foreseen the related consequences, they would not have given in. No doubt, Hagrid later wished he had stopped to think more clearly about what might have been going on behind the scenes and what might be at stake. His lapse left Harry's life in danger, his reputation and the continuance of Hogwarts at risk. Indeed, all he held dear in his own life, in his community, and in the larger battle being waged between good and evil was impacted because he was outwitted by Professor Quirrell's scheme. We can learn a lot by reflecting on the dangerous designs of the dragon-egg dealer.

The Quest for the Sorcerer's Stone

"The Sorcerer's Stone [is] a legendary substance with astonishing powers. The stone will transform any metal into pure gold. It also produces the Elixir of Life, which will make the drinker immortal."
—Hermione reading from a library book,
Book One, p. 220

*O*n the first day Harry entered the magical world, someone tried to steal the Sorcerer's Stone from Gringotts. That stirred up Harry's curiosity. But Harry, Ron, and Hermione's interest became urgent once Harry realized who was trying to steal the stone and why.

While Harry was in the Forbidden Forest trying to find out what had been killing the unicorns, he was helped by Firenze the centaur. Firenze pointed out, "Only one who has nothing to lose, and everything to gain, would commit such a crime" (Book One, p. 258). After that conversation, Harry realized that Voldemort was trying to steal the Sorcerer's Stone. The wealth and immortality it could produce (through the Elixir of Life) would allow him to return to power. Then he could once again destroy all that was good and dominate the wizarding world.

Harry then correctly understood that this was a matter of life and death, good versus evil. Therefore, he determined to fight—to the death, if necessary—to keep those on Voldemort's side from getting the stone. When Hermione tried to dissuade him, he pointed out that he was not worried about being expelled. If he failed, there would not be a Hogwarts to get expelled from. The Dark Lord would destroy it or turn it into a school for the Dark Arts. Harry knew that letting evil prevail would leave those on the side of good in mortal danger. Whoever was trying to get the Stone for Voldemort must be stopped.

In the opening pages of the Bible we read about a tree of life, one that could grant immortality (similar to the Elixir of Life). When Adam and Eve were deceived by the serpent and ate from the forbidden tree of the knowledge of good and evil, they fell under the curse of death. Then God drove them out of the garden of Eden. He also stationed an angel with a flaming sword to keep anyone from eating of the tree of life. Why? Perhaps having immortality before one has a remedy for the curse of sin and death would be terrible. So God made sure people could not have that which would give them immortality until he had rid the world of evil (see Gen. 3).

God did not want to keep people from having immortality; he created us to share eternity with him. God had to make sure that immortality would be free of the corruption and living death that came as a result of the fall. Jesus came to Earth to solve that problem. He also knew that the evil one who showed up as the serpent in the garden of Eden had sent false teachers to keep people from recognizing him and his mission. Jesus said, "The thief comes only to steal and kill and destroy" (John 10:10a).

In both Harry Potter's story and the Christian story, the villain has the same aims. Professor Quirrell was a false teacher who came to steal the Sorcerer's Stone, kill Harry, and destroy all that was good when Voldemort returned to power. However, those on the side of good set themselves against these aims. Jesus went on to say, "I came that they may have life, and have it abundantly" (John 10:10b).

God is not trying to keep us from immortality, but to let us have it when we are ready for it. Even Dumbledore showed concern over people using the Stone to have as much life and money as they wanted. He saw to it that the Sorcerer's Stone was destroyed, but we get the idea that he is not opposed to immortality. He did make sure Harry understood that there was a way in which death was not the end, but "the next great adventure" (Book One, p. 297). We do not know the end of Harry's story yet, but we can read the end of our story in the Bible. Humanity will not be deprived of immortality. Once sin, death, and evil are out of the way, God says, "To everyone who conquers, I will give permission to eat from the tree of life that is in the paradise of God" (Rev. 2:7). Then we won't need the Sorcerer's Stone to live forever; the paradise God promises gives eternal life and everlasting riches.

Harry, Ron, and Hermione's Soft Landing

"I know what this is—it's Devil's Snare!"
—Hermione to Harry and Ron, Book One, p. 277

*H*arry, Ron, and Hermione were racing to reach the Sorcerer's Stone before someone on Voldemort's side could lay hold of it and use its powers for evil. They had to get past Fluffy, through the trap door, and past all the enchantments guarding the Stone. When they dropped into the darkness through the trap door, Harry and Ron were relieved to land on a soft, comfortable plant. They thought themselves lucky that it was there. Only Hermione recognized the danger they were in, and pulled free of the entangling plant immediately before it could get a hold on her.

Harry and Ron were not as attentive in Herbology class as Hermione, nor were they aware of what was really happening while they made themselves comfortable. The plant that promised comfort was entwining its tendrils around them, clinging dangerously to them, and entangling them so that they could not escape. Only Hermione knew that it was Devil's Snare. A soft landing, a gradual entangling, a deadly end so that the race is never finished.

The Bible speaks of sin in the same way. Our lives are like a race, where the forces of evil are also on the move in our world. Even when we are endeavoring to do good or work against the larger evil, we can fall into "Devil's Snare." Think of the "little sins" we settle into ever so comfortably: the little lie that covers our shame or keeps us out of trouble, the way we slip right into gossip, the temporary exhilaration of alcohol and recreational drugs, or the sensual pleasures of sexual sin. The initial benefits or pleasures of sin are the devil's snare *because* they offer temporary comforts; otherwise, who would settle into such a thing? The Bible does not deny that sin indeed holds out temporary pleasures. Moses is commended for "choosing rather to share ill-treatment with the people of God than to enjoy the fleeting pleasures of sin" (Heb. 11:25).

As soon as Harry, Ron, and Hermione landed, Devil's Snare began immediately—although almost imperceptibly—to wrap its tendrils around them. So too with all of us who may fall into a situation we did not anticipate where sin is waiting with quickly entangling tendrils. Hermione made the right move—away from the Devil's Snare the instant she landed in it. The Letter to the Hebrews urges, "Let us throw off everything that hinders and the sin that so easily entangles, and let us run with perseverance the race marked out for us" (Heb. 12:1–2 NIV).

The race of life, toward the good ends God intends for us, is always hindered by and sometimes stopped whenever we settle into sin, whose nature is such that it easily entangles. Therefore, we need to throw it off quickly and repeatedly whenever we fall into it. If we settle down for too long, it eventually becomes deadly—to soul and spirit if not to life itself. Solomon wisely put it this way, "Sometimes there is a way that seems to be right, but in the end it is the way to death" (Prov. 16:25).

We can also take a lesson from Hermione's knowledge of the plant. Devil's Snare thrives in the dark. Therefore, Hermione was able to defeat it with light. God's remedy is similar for avoiding and defeating any snare of the devil: "God is light and in him there is no darkness at all. If we say that we have fellowship with him while we are walking in darkness, we lie and do not do what is true; but if we walk in the light as he himself is in the light, we have fellowship with one another, and the blood of Jesus his Son cleanses us from all sin" (1 John 1:5–7).

If Harry and Ron had remained comfortably resting in Devil's Snare, they would have died. They needed to get into the light, and to get out of that snare. Likewise, people need to become alert to the fact that their sins—perhaps especially the most comforting ones—may be a snare of the devil to lull them into a cozy place in the dark where no one will see their sins, but where they are destined to die if they do not break free. It is the light and truth of Jesus Christ that is able to set us free.

This Isn't Magic, It's Logic!

*"Brilliant," said Hermione. "This isn't magic—it's logic—
a puzzle. A lot of the greatest wizards haven't got an ounce
of logic, they'd be stuck in here forever."*
—Hermione to Harry, Book One, p. 285

*H*emione is the logical one of the group; she studies hard and uses her mind to benefit her friends. When she and Harry made their way past the living game of chess, they entered a room where seven bottles sat on a table. Each of the two doors was filled with flames they could not pass. A roll of paper next to the bottles explained that one would allow the drinker to move forward, one would transport the drinker back, two were harmless, and three held deadly poison. The riddle gave enough information for anyone who used logic to figure out which were which.

Hermione was relieved. Harry was afraid they would be stuck in there forever. Hermione thought it through and was confident she knew which bottles they should choose. They decided that Harry would proceed while Hermione went back to get Ron and summon Dumbledore. Hermione discounted her contribution as "Books! And cleverness!" admiring Harry's friendship and bravery more, but her logic played a vital part in their quest.

A lawyer asked Jesus, "Teacher, which commandment in the law is the greatest?" Jesus replied, "'You shall love the Lord your God

with all your heart, and with all your soul, and *with all your mind.*'
This is the greatest and first commandment. And a second is like it:
'You shall love your neighbor as yourself'" (Matt. 22:36–39).
Some people seem to think that loving God is something that
requires one to leave logic and intellect out of the process. In his
reply to the lawyer, Jesus indicated that this is not so.

On the other hand, just as Hermione's use of logic by itself was
not enough to get them all the way through, neither can one fully
comprehend God and the things of the spiritual realm by a purely
rational evaluation. Other elements come into play, not the least of
which is faith, but also a willingness to do God's will. However,
for the one who puts a lot of stock in things making sense logically,
God has provided enough to satisfy an intelligent examination of
the claims of Christ and the Bible. For example, the book of Acts
says that after Jesus' suffering "he presented himself alive to them
by *many convincing proofs,* appearing to them during forty days
and speaking about the kingdom of God" (Acts 1:3).

The four Gospels and the book of Acts are firsthand accounts of
eyewitnesses or those who interviewed eyewitnesses. The details
given are set in history, and are able to be considered logically as
one would consider any other historical testimony. These things
took place at specific places, at specific times, so the seeker can
check to see how well the accounts of Jesus' life and ministry line
up with history, archaeology, and with one's sense of reason. Those
who have never considered Christianity to be logical would do
well to read Josh McDowell's *The New Evidence That Demands a
Verdict,* Lee Strobel's *The Case for Christ,* William Lane Craig's
Reasonable Faith, or J. P. Moreland's *Scaling the Secular City.*[3]

Hermione had taken time to study and to sharpen her skills in
logic. This preparation enabled her to confidently choose the only
bottles that would get her and Harry safely through the flames and
free them from being trapped. Likewise, those who want to safely
escape fiery spiritual dangers and not live their lives trapped in a
spiritual quandry would do well to resort to using logic even in spiritual pursuits. Like Hermione, we will need to study and apply our
minds to considering the many convincing proofs God has provided
in the Bible and in the life, death, and resurrection of Jesus Christ.

Professor Quirrell's Defense Against the Dark Arts Lessons

"Next to [Snape], who would suspect p-p-poor, st-stuttering, P-Professor Quirrell?"
—Professor Quirrell to Harry, Book One, p. 288

*E*very reader of Harry Potter quickly learns to be alert to deception. Not everyone is what he or she appears to be. The first stark realization of this comes at the end of Book One, with the unveiling of Professor Quirrell's true nature and aims. As the Defense Against the Dark Arts teacher at Hogwarts, Quirrell was supposed to teach students to defend themselves against evil. He feigned timidity and nervousness, supposedly having been frightened during his studies while fending off forces of darkness. However, his friendliness toward Harry and his skittishness were a cover for a ruthless determination to kill Harry and do whatever was necessary to return Lord Voldemort to power.

Harry, Ron, and Hermione knew someone was trying to hurt Harry, steal the Stone, and restore Voldemort, but they targeted the "obvious" suspect, Professor Snape. His overt hatred of Harry, dark countenance, and ominous presence led to assumptions that caused them to totally misjudge the situation and people involved. This left them vulnerable to the real danger that was carefully disguised.

In the end, even though Professor Quirrell's classes did not teach much about really defending against the Dark Arts, his life became an object lesson of a warning in the Bible to protect oneself from evil. Jesus said, "Watch out for false prophets. They come to you in sheep's clothing, but inwardly they are ferocious wolves. By their fruit you will recognize them. Do people pick grapes from thornbushes, or figs from thistles? Likewise every good tree bears good fruit, but a bad tree bears bad fruit" (Matt. 7:15–17).

Professor Quirrell was not recognized immediately for what he was because fruit takes time to grow; thus, his evil plans remained concealed until they reached fruition. Down in the dungeons, when he thought he had Harry trapped and intended to kill him, Quirrell revealed that he had been the one to let the troll in during the Halloween feast. He had tried to knock Harry off his broom during the Quidditch match, while—astonishingly—Professor Snape was trying to protect Harry. Quirrell was the one who had broken into Gringotts in a vain attempt to steal the Sorcerer's Stone, and had continued trying to steal it so he could give his master the wealth, power, and immortality it promised. He was the one who had been killing the unicorns and drinking their blood. Why? Because *inwardly* he was a ferocious wolf, although he clothed himself in a sheepish, seemingly harmless manner. This is in keeping with the nature of evil; it sets out to accomplish dark deeds by way of deception. Therefore, to defend against the Dark Arts, one must remain alert to deception and understand that people are not always what they present themselves to be.

Hagrid's Remorse

"I told the evil git how ter get past Fluffy! I told him! . . . Yeh could've died! All fer a dragon egg! I'll never drink again!"

—Hagrid to Harry, Book One, p. 303

*O*nce Hagrid realized that his lapse had put Harry in danger, he was distraught. He burst into tears when he came to see Harry in the hospital. He accepted full responsibility for what he had done wrong. He admitted that his drunkenness and giving in to his weaknesses and desire for an illegal dragon egg put him at fault. He declared that he would never drink again. He felt so guilty that he was harder on himself than others were. He was overcome with grief and remorse.

While the Bible does not forbid drinking, it says, "Wine is a mocker and beer a brawler; whoever is led astray by them is not wise" (Prov. 20:1 NIV). It says, in effect, "Do not get drunk," which is related then to making unwise decisions and to an awareness that we live in times when evil is at large (Eph. 5:15–18). The Bible also says, "Conduct yourselves wisely toward outsiders, making the most of the time. Let your speech always be gracious, seasoned with salt, so that you may know how you ought to answer everyone" (Col. 4:5–6). Hagrid came to realize that his drinking let the evil one get the advantage, that he did not conduct himself wisely toward the stranger, and that he was not careful about how he answered him.

Hagrid may not have handled himself well with the stranger, but he handled his sins in exactly the right way! He came to the ones he had hurt, and confessed with heartfelt remorse. He willingly repented and declared his determination never to do it again. The Bible says, "If we say that we have no sin, we deceive ourselves, and the truth is not in us. If we confess our sins, he who is faithful and just will forgive us our sins and cleanse us from all unrighteousness. If we say that we have not sinned, we make him a liar, and his word is not in us" (1 John 1:8–10). Hagrid would be in good shape.

Some might argue that Hagrid does drink again in subsequent books. I have even heard one person say, "Hagrid is drunk in every scene." This is not true. Even though we see Hagrid drinking later, we see his heart in this scene. Moreover, we do not see a repeat of overt drunkenness. However, the Bible is very gracious to people who fall repeatedly into the same pattern of sin, as is recorded in the Psalms:

> The LORD is compassionate and gracious,
>   slow to anger, abounding in love.
> He will not always accuse,
>   nor will he harbor his anger forever;
> he does not treat us as our sins deserve
>   or repay us according to our iniquities.
> For as high as the heavens are above the earth,
>   so great is his love for those who fear him;
> as far as the east is from the west,
>   so far has he removed our transgressions from us.
> As a father has compassion on his children,
>   so the LORD has compassion on those who fear him;
> for he knows how we are formed,
>   he remembers that we are dust.
>
> (Ps. 103:8–14 NIV)

When Peter came to Jesus to ask how many times he had to forgive someone who repeated the same offense, he thought he was being generous when he suggested, "Up to seven times?" No doubt he was staggered when Jesus replied, "Not seven times, but seventy-seven times" (Matt. 18:21–22).

Harry responded to Hagrid's remorse beautifully. He forgave him without a second thought, and even comforted him. For the Christian, such forgiveness may not come as easily as it came to Harry, but it is not optional. Jesus made it clear that his followers must forgive from their hearts (see Matt. 18:35). We also see that receiving forgiveness does not encourage further sin for one who is rightly corrected. No doubt, Hagrid would be less likely to fall into such behavior again because he was instructed by the consequences of his actions. (Still, although true biblical forgiveness can bring reconciliation, it does not remove the subsequent consequences of wrongdoing. One can be sorry and be forgiven, but one must still live with the consequences.)

Hagrid and Harry act as good models of how to repent of sin and to seek and extend forgiveness. The reconciliation, comfort, and restored relationship between Hagrid and Harry is a high point of Book One. These also highlight the new life God wants us to enjoy in his kingdom. The "gospel" is good news because it brings reconciliation, comfort, and restored relationship between people, but also in our relationship with God himself.

Harry's Battle with the Dark Lord

"See what I have become?" the face said. "Mere shadow and vapor . . . I have form only when I can share another's body . . . but there have always been those willing to let me into their hearts and minds."
— Voldemort to Harry, Book One, p. 293

*W*hen Harry came face to face with Voldemort, he learned that he had become a disembodied spirit, forced to work through others by taking up residence in them. Harry resisted the evil one, and after the battle—which left Harry unconscious and Quirrell mortally wounded—the evil spirit fled.

Later, when discussing the whole battle with Ron and Hermione, Harry contemplated how he had come to have the confrontation with Voldemort. He thought that Dumbledore wanted to give him a chance to face Voldemort himself. He recalled how he had learned to use the Mirror of Erised, with the help of the Invisibility Cloak provided by Dumbledore, and figured it was no accident. He said, "I think he knows more or less everything that goes on here, you know. I reckon he had a pretty good idea we were going to try, and instead of stopping us, he just taught us enough to help" (Book One, p. 302).

There are several similarities between Harry's encounter with Voldemort and things the Bible teaches about our interaction with the evil spiritual forces at work in this world. The Bible speaks of disembodied spirits that can come into a person and take over. Sometimes we see that these evil spirits were just filling a spiritual void, taking possession of that person without the person's consent. But there are also spiritual forces that are identified as being behind the destructive belief systems of false prophets. These take hold of persons when they willingly open their hearts and minds to a spirit other than the Holy Spirit of God. We guard against these by refusing to believe their false teachings. It was in the battle for the heart and mind that Harry won the battle, and Quirrell lost it.

The apostle John wrote a warning to early Christians that still applies today:

> Dear friends, do not believe every spirit, but test the spirits to see whether they are from God, because many false prophets have gone out into the world. This is how you can recognize the Spirit of God: Every spirit that acknowledges that Jesus Christ has come in the flesh is from God, but every spirit that does not acknowledge Jesus is not from God. This is the spirit of the antichrist, which you have heard is coming and even now is already in the world. (1 John 4:1–3 NIV)

Some may think it strange that God does not simply do away with the evil one, since he has the power and knows all that is going on, but for some reason God has chosen to give people the opportunity to fight the evil one and—hopefully—win. To this end he instructs us: "Submit yourselves therefore to God. Resist the devil, and he will flee from you" (Jas. 4:7). Seeing how the "shadow and vapor" that Voldemort had become fled from Harry after he resisted giving in to evil can serve to remind us of this promise.

Why the Evil One Could Not Touch Harry

"Love as powerful as your mother's for you leaves its own mark. Not a scar, no visible sign . . . to have been loved so deeply, even though the person who loved us is gone, will give us some protection forever."
—Dumbledore to Harry, Book One, p. 299

*H*arry was surprised to find that Quirrell could not bear to touch him without great pain and injury to himself. When he asked Dumbledore about it, the answer all came down to the power of love. The love of Harry's mother when she gave her life for him not only spared him from death, it left him with an invisible protection. The extent of this protection is still a mystery, but its source is clear.

As Lily Potter's act of self-sacrificial love saved Harry from the curse of death and made it so that the evil one could not touch him, the Bible says that those who are born of God through faith in the self-sacrificial death of Christ have a special protection. The reality that the "whole world lies under the power of the evil one" does not negate this. The Bible promises those who are born of God that "the one who was born of God protects them, and the evil one does not touch them" (1 John 5:18). However, it also acknowledges that we live in a world dominated by evil. That same passage goes on to say, "We know that we are God's children, and that the whole world lies under the power of the evil one" (1 John 5:19).

Harry's protection against his evil foe, received as a result of his mother's love, can remind us of the protection God offers his children in a world where we too come under the attack of our evil foe.

A Last-Minute Change of Decorations

[Dumbledore] clapped his hands. In an instant, the green hangings became scarlet and the silver became gold; the huge Slytherin serpent vanished and a towering Gryffindor lion took its place.

—Book One, p. 306

While Harry and his friends were busy trying to save the wizarding world, Slytherin was still far ahead in points to win the house cup. As the students came together for the end-of-term awards banquet, it looked like Slytherin had won. The Great Hall was decorated with the silver and green banner of Slytherin, bearing the symbol of the snake. The Slytherins were celebrating, but there was to be a sudden turn of fortunes.

Professor Dumbledore awarded points to Ron, Hermione, Harry, and Neville for their respective demonstrations of intelligence and courage. At the last moment, the silver and green banners of Slytherin bearing the snake were replaced with the red and gold banners of Gryffindor bearing the lion. Slytherins who had been rejoicing a moment before fell silent; Gryffindors who had been subdued were suddenly cheering.

Sometimes it looks like evil is winning, but things can change suddenly. God is the only one who knows everything that is going on, and he keeps the score. Jesus tried to explain this to his disciples so they would not get discouraged:

49

I tell you the truth, you will weep and mourn while the world rejoices. You will grieve, but your grief will turn to joy. A woman giving birth to a child has pain because her time has come; but when her baby is born she forgets the anguish because of her joy that a child is born into the world. So with you: Now is your time of grief, but I will see you again and you will rejoice, and no one will take away your joy. (John 16:20–22 NIV)

When Jesus was crucified, his disciples wept and the world rejoiced. Even though Jesus had forewarned them, they thought the contest was over and that evil had won. But Jesus had a few points to give them. When he did, it only took an instant for their grief to turn to joy as they realized their side was victorious. In Luke 24:13–35, two of Jesus' followers are walking along, discussing the recent events, when the risen Jesus begins to walk with them. They do not recognize him, however, and begin to tell him the story of the crucifixion. Then they stop to eat. "When he was at the table with them, he took bread, blessed and broke it, and gave it to them. Then their eyes were opened, and they recognized him; and he vanished from their sight. They said to each other, 'Were not our hearts burning within us while he was talking to us on the road, while he was opening the scriptures to us?'" (Luke 24:30–32).

Even now, with the terrorism, wars, and poverty in our world, it may seem that evil has the upper hand. However, we are called to act like Harry and his friends did and to keep focused on fighting evil, even if it seems like evil is winning. Things can change suddenly in such battles. When it comes down to the final battle and the final prizes are awarded, God says there will be an upset. The Bible says that the world will get worse and worse, but that an instant will come when Christ will return, evil will be put down, and all those on God's side will celebrate like never before.

Glimmers of the Gospel in Book Two

Harry Potter and the Chamber of Secrets

Introduction to Book Two

*B*ook Two's predominant themes are freedom for those held captive or enslaved, and the rejection of prejudice and hatred on the basis of bloodline. Another prominent theme is that whatever you send out will come back on you in like kind. Book Two so richly weaves these themes throughout the book that I consider it very sad that many Christians who are working diligently to eradicate racial hatred and bigotry do not even know that these are primary themes throughout the series.

I was interviewed on the radio by a highly respected African-American woman who carries substantial influence within the Christian community. Before having me on to discuss Harry Potter, her staff spent several hours trying to track down a woman who had been quoted in a piece about Harry Potter leading children into Satanism. They were unable to locate her, so the host asked me if I knew her. I told them the article they had received was quoted from the satirical Web site *The Onion,* and that the "quotes" were from fictitious people.

We all laughed, but there was an undercurrent of discomfort that such a fabricated story had been passed along as fact and adapted in such a way that many otherwise credible Christians were believing it and persuading others to believe it. I followed this by asking the host if anyone had made her aware that the books carry a warning of the dangers and destructiveness of hatred and bigotry on the basis of bloodline, as well as strong themes about eradicating slavery and oppression. She had never heard any mention of those themes that were close to her heart as a Christian and as an African-American woman.

Let me summarize some of these themes from Book Two. First comes the theme of freedom for those who are enslaved and oppressed. The book starts with Harry being forced to pretend that he does not even exist, then being imprisoned in his own bedroom by the Dursleys. Harry is freed by Fred, George, and Ron. Throughout the book we see the suffering of Dobby the house-elf as a perpetual slave to the house of Malfoy from generation to generation, and how Dobby is finally freed by Harry's act of redemption. We also see how Ginny is taken captive by Tom Riddle. She becomes enslaved within that relationship, falls under his influence, and becomes a slave to her own sins and the secrecy created by trying to cover up what she has done. She ends up being taken captive by Tom down in the Chamber of Secrets. The climax of the story comes when Harry and Ron risk their lives to free her. In all these ways, we see the dangers and destructiveness of oppression countered with the efforts of others to set the captives free and eradicate oppression wherever it is imposed.

A secondary theme in Book Two is that it is not right to be prejudiced against others on the basis of their bloodline; one should discriminate—in the healthy sense of the word—on the basis of what a person has chosen to become. We see this in the hatred against those born of Muggle parents or of mixed heritage and in the outrage of good students against the use of the word "Mudblood" as a racial slur. The book also explores the history of such bigotry. Those on the good side rejected this belief promoted by Salazar Slytherin and split from him over it.

Another secondary theme in Book Two is that one must be careful what one dishes out to others because it could come right back at oneself (nicely contrived with a broken wand that sends the curse meant for another back on the sender). Gilderoy Lockhart made his reputation by using the Memory Charm to remove the memories of those whose knowledge and expertise he had appropriated as his own. When he tried to use the Memory Charm on Harry and Ron, it rebounded on him.

Ron was delighted to see this happen to Professor Lockhart because he saw through Lockhart from the beginning. But Ron had no room to gloat, for he also had an experience of getting back precisely what he aimed at someone else. When he tried to use his wand to make Draco Malfoy belch up slugs, he was hit with the curse instead, which left him belching the slugs he had intended for his enemy. This is a novel way of saying what Jesus said: "So in everything, do to others what you would have them do to you, for this sums up the Law and the Prophets" (Matt. 7:12 NIV).

Mr. Weasley's Loophole
in Magical Law

"Yeah, Dad's crazy about everything to do with Muggles;
our shed's full of Muggle stuff. He takes it apart, puts
spells on it, and puts it back together again. If he raided
our *house he'd have to put himself under arrest."*
—Fred Weasley to Harry, Book Two, p. 31

*B*ook Two begins with Dobby's warning and the incident with
Aunt Petunia's pudding. As punishment, Harry was held captive in
his bedroom at the Dursleys'. Ron was concerned because Harry
had not responded to any of his letters. Then Fred, George, and
Ron learned that Harry had received a warning from the Ministry
of Magic for using magic in front of Muggles, so they came to
check on him. They "borrowed" Mr. Weasley's flying car, although
flying it violated wizarding law, but when they found Harry locked
in his bedroom with bars on the window, they felt justified. After
they rescued Harry, they chided him for doing magic in front of
Muggles (missing the irony entirely), but he insisted that he had
not done so. He also rightly pointed out that they had no place to
talk, given that they were driving a flying car!

The fact that Mr. Weasley worked in the Misuse of Muggle Artifacts Office and had an enchanted car only heightened the irony.
Given his enthusiasm for "Muggle stuff," it seems Mr. Weasley
could not resist breaking the very laws he was committed to uphold-
ing. Even though the Weasley boys justified their behavior to themselves, Mrs. Weasley did not share their view. They got in plenty of
trouble when they arrived home and found her waiting for them.
Mrs. Weasley also confronted Mr. Weasley about his flying car.

Mr. Weasley admitted that it was "very wrong indeed" for the boys to fly the car. When Mrs. Weasley pointed the finger at him, he pointed out that there was a loophole in the law so that he could *have* a flying car as long as he was not *intending* to fly it. Mrs. Weasley was obviously unimpressed by this technicality.

This episode is quite revealing, not only about how Fred, George, and even Mr. Weasley attempt to justify their misdeeds to themselves (as we all tend to do) but also how it relates to the universal human need to satisfy the law, while escaping the prescribed judgment against breaking God's law. In religious terms, this has to do with finding atonement for sin.

Before a person can look for a way to get out of deserved punishment, he must realize that he has been convicted. The Letter to the Romans leads up to this point in an inescapable way. It starts by convincing the reader that God's being is self-evident, except to those who choose to believe a lie (which conveniently releases them from any moral obligation to God in their own minds). Then it points to the more obvious and less socially acceptable sins (rightly presuming that those who are inclined toward more socially acceptable sins will condemn those they deem worse sinners than themselves). Then comes the twist that catches everyone in the net.

Addressing the teachers of the law, the apostle Paul asks, "You, then, that teach others, will you not teach yourself? While you preach against stealing, do you steal? You that forbid adultery, do you commit adultery? You that abhor idols, do you rob temples? You that boast in the law, do you dishonor God by breaking the law?" (Rom. 2:21–23). Surely any individual reading that passage would not have broken all these laws, but in going through a laundry list of the things we know are legally right, all of us will come to realize our own guilt on some point. As the Letter of James concludes, "For whoever keeps the whole law but fails in one point has become accountable for all of it" (Jas. 2:10).

What is the Bible getting at that is similar to what Mr. Weasley

did? Those who prided themselves on teaching the law and hold-
ing others accountable were not better than those they looked
down on as "sinners." Everyone is shown to be "under the power
of sin" (Rom. 3:9) "so that every mouth may be silenced, and the
whole world may be held accountable to God. For 'no human
being will be justified in his sight' by deeds prescribed by the law,
for through the law comes the knowledge of sin" (Rom. 3:19–20).

Once a person recognizes his or her own sin, that person must
find a loophole or die. The Bible says the punishment for sin is
death, followed by the wrath of God being unleashed against all
who have sin held to their account. This is a disturbing thought
because the Bible also says that God is love. How can a loving and
holy God satisfy his love for people who break his law and main-
tain justice? The spiritual "loophole" Christians rely on is found in
the doctrine of atonement.

Throughout the Old Testament, God made provision for sins to
be covered with the shed blood of animal sacrifices. Each year the
Jewish law allowed people to assign their sin to a scapegoat, which
was set free to carry their sins away. Also, the high priest would
offer the blood of animals to atone for his own sin and the sins of
the people (see the instructions given to Moses in Lev. 16). The
sacrifices for atonement of sin were taken into the temple in Jerusalem, into the Most Holy Place, where God's presence resided
over the Ark of the Covenant (which held the Ten Command-
ments). If God accepted their sacrifice, their sins were covered for
another year. In this way, the people could escape their due punishment for sin while still acknowledging that God is just and his
law righteous (even though they were not).

I believe that God ingeniously planned all along to send Jesus,
holy and sinless, to shed his blood on the cross to pay our penalty
for sin once and for all. (The Letter to the Hebrews explains this in
detail.) Therefore, the penalty is paid, and those who put their faith
in the atoning power of the blood of Jesus can be spared the due
punishment of death, God's wrath, and eternal separation from our
righteous God.

The New Testament asserts that this "loophole" is the only one
left open, and that there is no longer any need to go back year after

year: "For it was fitting that we should have such a high priest, holy, blameless, undefiled, separated from sinners, and exalted above the heavens. Unlike the other high priests, he has no need to offer sacrifices day after day, first for his own sins, and then for those of the people; this he did once for all when he offered himself" (Heb. 7:26–27).

Consider also Paul's understanding of this new reality:

> But now, apart from law, the righteousness of God has been disclosed, and is attested by the law and the prophets, the righteousness of God through faith in Jesus Christ for all who believe. For there is no distinction, since all have sinned and fall short of the glory of God; they are now justified by his grace as a gift, through the redemption that is in Christ Jesus, whom God put forward as a sacrifice of atonement by his blood, effective through faith. He did this to show his righteousness, because in his divine forbearance he had passed over the sins previously committed; it was to prove at the present time that he himself is righteous and that he justifies the one who has faith in Jesus. (Rom. 3: 21–26)

In everyday terms, the discussion between Mr. and Mrs. Weasley can be seen as a model of the outworking of the spiritual implication that flows from the doctrine of atonement. In ancient Israel, the Day of Atonement was a day of solemn reflection, of sorrow over and repentance from sin—even though the people received God's covering for sin. Atonement was never meant to give them license to break God's law. Those who now trust in Christ's blood as their atoning sacrifice have remission of sins and forgiveness for their infractions of the law, but this should never be used as license to sin. Similarly, Mrs. Weasley's heartfelt conviction that the loophole in the law was not to be used as license to condone law-breaking is a necessary balance to Mr. Weasley's overreliance on it. The balance they strike in this conversation is at the heart of living out the gospel life.

The Mystery of the
Shrinking Door Keys

"Of course, it's very hard to convict anyone because no Muggle would admit their key keeps shrinking—they'll insist they just keep losing it. Bless them, they'll go to any lengths to ignore magic, even if it's staring them in the face."

—Mr. Weasley, Book Two, p. 38

*M*r. Weasley had been out all night on raids looking for Muggle artifacts that had been enchanted. Upon coming home, he told his family and Harry, "All I got were a few shrinking door keys and a biting kettle." Mr. Weasley complained that it was hard to get convictions because Muggles "go to any lengths to ignore magic, even if it's staring them in the face."

If one thinks of the kind of magic in Harry Potter's world as representing miracles in our own, this comment points to something of note about people's response to Jesus. Any cursory reading of the Gospels reveals that Jesus went about openly doing things that were clearly miraculous. In broad daylight, in front of large crowds, Jesus made blind people see, caused the deaf to hear, restored withered limbs, cleansed lepers of their dreaded skin disease, caused the lame to walk, even raised the dead—all right before their eyes!

Most people marveled and gave thanks to God. His enemies, however, seemed to be blind to what he was doing. Technically, they saw what he did. Sometimes they would even argue with him because he was doing these miracles on the Sabbath day, which—in their minds—constituted work and was a violation of religious interpretations of God's law. But they refused to admit that his miraculous power was a sign from God, even though it was staring them in the face!

One time a huge crowd saw Jesus feed thousands, themselves included, with a little boy's lunch. Soon after, they said, "What sign will you show us so that we may believe in you?" *What sign?* Jesus rightly answered that he would give them "the sign of Jonah." This meant that he would die and be resurrected three days later, similar to how Jonah went down into the depths and spent three days and three nights in the belly of a great fish. But even then Jesus knew they still would not believe.

Their spiritual blindness was astounding. On one occasion it was almost funny, if you think of what it must have been like among those discussing how to get rid of Jesus and his troublesome miracles. Near the culmination of Jesus' ministry, his friend Lazarus became sick and died. Friends and foes of Jesus came for the funeral, wondering aloud how Jesus could have let Lazarus die when he had healed so many others. Jesus finally showed up, four days after Lazarus had been put in the tomb—without being embalmed. Jesus publicly put an end to the mourning when he called Lazarus to come out. And Lazarus came out, alive from the dead! This sign was a demonstration of Jesus' proclamation, "I am the resurrection and the life. Those who believe in me, even though they die, will live, and everyone who lives and believes in me will never die" (John 11:25). Not surprisingly, this was an effective object lesson, and many believed in Jesus because of this miracle.

How did this impact those who had set themselves against Jesus (mostly religious leaders who were jealous of his following)? Did they say, "Wow! He must be the Son of God!"? No! Instead, they accelerated their plans to have Jesus arrested and killed. Here is the funny part that shows how they would go to any lengths to ignore the miraculous even when it was staring them in the face: While they plotted to have Jesus arrested and put to death, they planned to kill Lazarus too, even though he didn't stay dead the first time!

John's Gospel reports, "When the great crowd of the Jews learned that he was there, they came not only because of Jesus but also to see Lazarus, whom he had raised from the dead. So the chief priests planned to put Lazarus to death as well, since it was on account of him that many of the Jews were deserting and were believing in Jesus" (John 12:9–11).

After Jesus' crucifixion, the religious leaders were bombarded with inescapable miracles: The soldiers they had sent to guard Jesus' tomb came running back terrified because they had seen angels and Jesus' resurrection. The religious leaders had to pay them hush money. These leaders most likely felt the earthquake that occurred that morning. They could see that the curtain in the temple had been torn from top to bottom (signifying that the way was now open for people to come directly into God's presence). They may have seen or at least heard reports of saints of old who made appearances in Jerusalem at the time of the resurrection. With all of this staring them in the face, they somehow managed to ignore it all.

The Bible gives us an explanation for this: "In their case the god of this world has blinded the minds of the unbelievers, to keep them from seeing the light of the gospel of the glory of Christ, who is the image of God" (2 Cor. 4:4). In our world, the insistence on denying the miraculous has a more ominous source than what we see with the Muggles who refuse to admit that their door keys keep shrinking.

The Best Seeker Wins the Game

"This," *said Wood, "is the Golden Snitch, and it's the most important ball of the lot."*
—Oliver Wood to Harry, Book One, p. 169

When Oliver Wood explained Quidditch to Harry for the first time, he turned his attention to the Golden Snitch, stressing that it is very hard to catch because it is fast and difficult to see. But it was the Seeker's job to catch it. The Seeker had to keep seeking the Golden Snitch, even while weaving in and out of the Chasers, Beaters, Bludgers, and Quaffle to catch it before the other team's Seeker. Whichever Seeker caught the Snitch would win an extra hundred and fifty points for his or her team. Generally speaking, it is the team with the best Seeker that nearly always wins the game.

Let's consider a modern-day parable that relates to a Quidditch match in Harry's second year: The kingdom of heaven is like a Seeker (Harry) who goes out to play the most important game of the season—Gryffindor versus Slytherin, with Draco Malfoy playing Seeker for Slytherin. When he sees the Snitch he risks all to catch it, even though he has been hit by a rogue Bludger and one arm is broken. He darts after the Snitch, even taking both hands off his broom to catch it and win the game (see Matt. 13:45–46).

As a Seeker, Harry has a knack for spotting things other people do not, but he also devotes himself to training with all his heart and strength. God says, "When you search for me, you will find me; if you *seek me* with all your heart, I will let you find me, says the LORD" (Jer. 29:13). Such dedication is sure to pay off in spiritual and practical terms according to these promises made by Jesus: "But *seek* first [God's] kingdom and his righteousness, and all these things [food, clothing, etc.] will be given to you as well" (Matt. 6:33 NIV). "Ask and it will be given to you; *seek* and you will find; knock and the door will be opened to you. For everyone who asks receives; he who *seeks* finds; and to him who knocks, the door will be opened" (Matt. 7:7–8 NIV).

In life, as in a game of Quidditch, it is usually the best seekers who win the game.

You've Got to Make Some Sacrifices

"Harry Potter risks his own life for his friends!" moaned Dobby.
—Dobby the house-elf, Book Two, p. 179

*O*ne of the distinguishing characteristics of those in the house of Gryffindor in the Harry Potter stories is their willingness to make sacrifices for each other. This is certainly different from the Slytherins. As Book One begins, Lily Potter has just made the ultimate sacrifice by giving her life for Harry. Then when Harry, Ron, and Hermione reached the life-sized chess board in their search for the Sorcerer's Stone, Ron knew best how to play the game:

> "Yes . . ." said Ron softly, "it's the only way . . . I have got to be taken."
> "NO!" Harry and Hermione shouted.
> "That's chess!" snapped Ron. "You've got to make some sacrifices!" (Book One, p. 283)

As a knight, Ron let himself be taken by the white queen, not knowing if that would hurt, if it would knock him out, or if it would kill him. It certainly looked painful to be captured in a game of wizard's chess. He did know that it was the only way they could win, and therefore the only way his friends could proceed in their attempt to stop the thief and save the school.

In Book Two, Dobby the house-elf did all he could to get Harry to go home and avoid the mounting danger at Hogwarts. Dobby knew more than he could say, but there was a monster on the loose intent on killing Muggle-borns, which included Hermione. Harry ended up being hurt severely by a rogue Bludger—followed by having the bones in his arm regrown, thanks to Professor Lockhart's lame attempts to mend the broken bone. Nevertheless, Harry adamantly refused to go home when Dobby urged him to escape danger.

[Dobby squealed,] "Go home, Harry Potter, go home!"

"I'm not going anywhere!" said Harry fiercely. "One of my best friends is Muggle-born; she'll be first in line if the Chamber really has been opened—"

"Harry Potter risks his own life for his friends!" moaned Dobby. (Book Two, p. 179)

All of these are beautiful examples of the kind of friendship Jesus wanted to characterize his followers. Jesus told his disciples, "This is my commandment, that you love one another as I have loved you. No one has greater love than this, to lay down one's life for one's friends" (John 15:12–13). Jesus proved his friendship for us when he lay down his life for us on the cross. He knew it was the only way the game could be won. So when we think of those in Gryffindor House who willingly sacrifice for each other, let us not forget the greatest sacrifice of all, and determine to make sacrifices for our friends.

Pure-Bloods, Muggles, and Mudbloods

"What's the new password again?" he said to Harry.
"Er—" said Harry.
"Oh, yeah—pure-blood!" said Malfoy.
—Book Two, p. 221

*B*ook Two reveals the history of the bigotry among some in the wizarding world against Muggles and those who are the children of Muggles. It dates all the way back to one of the founders of Hogwarts, Salazar Slytherin. He believed that only "pure-bloods," those of purely wizarding parentage, should be allowed to study at Hogwarts. This difference of opinion between Slytherin and the other three founders created quite a rift. This tradition of bigotry became more pronounced through time, so that fifty years before Harry's time at Hogwarts, a monster released by the Heir of Slytherin killed a girl. In Book Two, that same monster was once again set loose to target "Mudbloods," a vulgar term for anyone not of pure wizarding family heritage.

Those who align themselves with Salazar Slytherin share his bigotry toward those who are not "pure-bloods," but also any who accept Muggle-borns and those of mixed parentage. We see this in Lucius Malfoy's comments to Mr. Weasley. The Weasleys have pure-wizarding ancestry, but they accept all students, regardless of their bloodline. Mr. Weasley's Muggle Protection Act seems to be the target of Mr. Malfoy's attempts to discredit the Weasley family. Some of the students in Slytherin House are openly bigoted, as Draco is to Hermione (whose parents are both Muggles). One might wonder if the Slytherins' bigotry goes beyond race to

67

include gender since there are no girls on the Slytherins' Quidditch team (although this may change in later books). We also see a measure of hatred and contempt toward those of lower social class or economic level among the Slytherins.

When we learn more about the Heir of Slytherin, it is interesting to note that he is actually not pure-blooded himself. He proudly states that he has the blood of Salazar Slytherin flowing through his veins on his mother's side, but that his father was a Muggle. Future books reveal the lengths to which his hatred of his Muggle parentage will take him. What is clearly seen in this story is that those following the Dark Lord have hatred toward others on the basis of their ancestry and bloodline, a murderous hatred!

Sadly, history reveals that some who have claimed to be Christians have practiced a kind of bigotry similar to that of Salazar Slytherin and his heir, even to the extreme of participating in the Nazi genocide on the basis of bloodline. Such genocidal bigotry can be found in other religious traditions and political regimes as well, where bigotry and hatred motivate killing others on the basis of ethnicity. Such murderous bigotry, seen as the outworking of evil in the Harry Potter stories, is contrary to the gospel message.

The Old Testament says, "[God] shows no partiality to nobles, nor regards the rich more than the poor, for they are all the work of his hands" (Job 34:19). Jesus stunned his disciples and the religious leaders by disregarding the accepted bigotry of his day. He offered the gift of God to a Samaritan woman. Samaritans were hated by most Jews, and this particular woman had also raised a few eyebrows by being married five times and living with a man who was not her husband. He did miracles for Gentiles as well as Jews, although he did acknowledge that his ministry to Jews came first. He allowed women to be his disciples and to listen to his teaching, contrary to other rabbis of the time. He welcomed the poor along with the rich. He lived out the pronouncement made throughout the Old and New Testaments that "God shows no partiality" (Rom. 2:11). (See Acts 10–11 for a story that reveals what a revolutionary concept this was, even to Jesus' disciples and the early church.)

The good news Jesus came to bring was revolutionary, in large measure because it took the promise of blessings God had made to Abraham and his seed (commonly thought to mean only the Jews) and threw the doors wide open for everyone who would believe in Jesus. The Letter to the Galatians sums it up this way: "There is no longer Jew or Greek, there is no longer slave or free, there is no longer male and female; for all of you are one in Christ Jesus. And if you belong to Christ, then you are Abraham's offspring, heirs according to the promise" (Gal. 3:28–29).

The book of Revelation includes a remarkable vision of heaven: "There was a great multitude that no one could count, from every nation, from all tribes and peoples and languages, standing before the throne and before the Lamb, robed in white, with palm branches in their hands" (Rev. 7:9). The only "pure blood" recognized by God is the blood of Jesus. That is the only password necessary to open the doors and gain admittance to the kingdom of heaven.

Professor Dumbledore's Parting Words

"However," said Dumbledore, speaking very slowly and clearly so that none of them could miss a word, "you will find that I will only truly have left this school when none here are loyal to me. You will also find that help will always be given at Hogwarts to those who ask for it."
—Dumbledore to Harry and Ron,
Book Two, pp. 263–64

When Hermione and Penelope Clearwater were petrified by the monster, everyone at Hogwarts became distressed. The school would be closed if the attacks did not stop. Tom Riddle had led Harry to suspect Hagrid, so at that point Ron and Harry took the Invisibility Cloak and went to Hagrid's hut. Hagrid greeted them with a crossbow, terribly nervous and expecting company. When a knock came at the door, Harry and Ron hid under the Invisibility Cloak while Dumbledore and Cornelius Fudge, Minister of Magic, entered. Over the protests of Dumbledore, Fudge had come to take Hagrid away to Azkaban as a precaution against future attacks.

The next knock brought Mr. Malfoy, who had managed to "persuade" the school governors to suspend Dumbledore as headmaster because he was unable to stop the attacks. At this Fudge exclaimed, "See here, Malfoy, if *Dumbledore* can't stop them . . . who *can*?" But Dumbledore remained calm and agreed to go away. However, he had some parting words that seemed to be intended for the boys hiding under the cloak. Much later, when Harry faced off with Tom Riddle, Tom bragged that Dumbledore had been driven from the school by the mere memory of him. Harry countered, "He's not as gone as you might think!" And just then, the music of the phoenix could be heard.

While Jesus was on earth, his disciples could go to him with all the problems they could not handle—which were plentiful. When the time came for Jesus to depart and go (back to the Father in heaven), he prepared his disciples to function in a new way. They were assured that even though he was gone, he was not really gone. Jesus promised that he was available to them whenever "two or three are gathered in my name"; those who took his name and remained loyal to him could trust that he was with them (Matt. 18:20). After he had risen from the dead, he gave them final instructions before ascending back into heaven: "All authority in heaven and on earth has been given to me. Go therefore and make disciples of all nations, baptizing them in the name of the Father and of the Son and of the Holy Spirit, and teaching them to obey everything that I have commanded you. *And remember, I am with you always, to the end of the age*" (Matt. 28:18–20).

Dumbledore's promise that help would be given at Hogwarts to all who ask for it is also reminiscent of something Jesus promised his followers: "Very truly, I tell you, if you ask anything of the Father in my name, he will give it to you. Until now you have not asked for anything in my name. Ask and you will receive, so that your joy may be complete" (John 16:23–24). The time came when Harry especially needed to know Dumbledore was not really gone, and when he needed to call out for help, which he did while fighting the basilisk.

Likewise, the real good news of the gospel is not that Jesus lived two thousand years ago, did amazing things we should remember, and was a remarkable moral teacher. The good news is that Jesus will only truly have left this world when none here are loyal to him (that is, when he takes them out). Even though we cannot see him bodily now, Jesus is here, and help will always be given to those who ask for it in his name.

Gilderoy Lockhart Goes Down!

"It's not all book signings and publicity photos, you know.
You want fame, you have to be prepared for a long hard
slog."
—Gilderoy Lockhart to Harry, Book Two, p. 298

Gilderoy Lockhart created quite a lofty reputation for himself, albeit by questionable means—but that seemed beside the point to Professor Lockhart. The entire collection of books he claimed to have authored was an assortment of the expertise, accomplishments, and conquests of others. Professor Lockhart appropriated these for himself, while looking down on those whose work he stole.

Lockhart viewed everything as an opportunity to exalt himself. At book signings, before the media, among the faculty at Hogwarts—Lockhart was puffed up with conceit. He created quite the image: winning *Witch Weekly*'s Most-Charming-Smile Award five times in a row, always dressed to color-coordinated perfection, with his hat set at a jaunty angle. Lockhart pursued the adulation of his fans, and was usually prepared to hand out autographed photos.

His elevated view of himself caused him to lose perspective, however. He claimed to know more than everyone else—Dumbledore included. He openly bragged that he knew where the Chamber of Secrets was hidden, and could have rid the school of the monster if he had been given free reign. He also assumed that Harry shared his quest for fame. This was not the case, as attested to by Harry's resistance to Colin Creevy's hero worship. In a flash of arrogance, Lockhart presumed Harry wanted to be just like him.

Lockhart told Harry, "Yes, yes, I know what you're thinking! 'It's all right for him, he's an internationally famous wizard already!' But when I was twelve, I was just as much of a nobody as you are now. In fact, I'd say I was even more of a nobody! I mean, a few people have heard of you, haven't they? All that business with He-Who-Must-Not-Be-Named!" (Book Two, p. 91).

The other professors knew Lockhart for the fraud he was, so when the monster had taken a student down into the Chamber of Secrets, they were delighted at the chance to bring him down a few pegs. Professor McGonagall's invitation for him to have free reign at catching the monster and saving the girl gave Lockhart's peers a measure of pleasure even in that dark moment. However, they had no idea how far down Professor Lockhart would be forced to go.

The Bible makes this declaration: "All who exalt themselves will be humbled, and all who humble themselves will be exalted" (Matt. 23:12). We can see this in a parable Jesus told to put people like Gilderoy Lockhart in their place:

> Two men went up to the temple to pray, one a Pharisee and the other a tax collector. The Pharisee, standing by himself, was praying thus, "God, I thank you that I am not like other people: thieves, rogues, adulterers, or even like this tax collector. I fast twice a week; I give a tenth of all my income." But the tax collector, standing far off, would not even look up to heaven, but was beating his breast and saying, "God, be merciful to me, a sinner!" I tell you, this man went down to his home justified rather than the other; for all who exalt themselves will be humbled, but all who humble themselves will be exalted. (Luke 18:10–14)

Another parallel in looking at what happened to Gilderoy Lockhart speaks more directly to the gospel message. Professor Lockhart, who exalted himself, was indeed humbled. He was brought down not only figuratively but literally when Ron and Harry forced him to go down far under the school, into the Chamber of

Secrets. Once there, Lockhart got exactly what was coming to him. When he tried to cast his Memory Charm on Ron and Harry, it came back on him.

Gilderoy Lockhart exalted himself and was brought down, but this story also shows that those who humble themselves will be lifted. Harry and Ron (who had been humble all along and willingly lowered themselves into the depths under the school to save Ginny) were raised up by the phoenix. After being raised up, they were honored by Dumbledore. Both received Special Awards for Service to the School and two hundred points apiece for Gryffindor. This could serve to illustrate a theme taught in the book of Philippians:

> Do nothing from selfish ambition or conceit, but in humility regard others as better than yourselves. Let each of you look not to your own interests, but to the interests of others. Let the same mind be in you that was in Christ Jesus,
>
> who, though he was in the form of God,
>   did not regard equality with God
>   as something to be exploited,
> but emptied himself,
>   taking the form of a slave,
>   being born in human likeness.
> And being found in human form,
>   he humbled himself
>   and became obedient to the point of death—
>   even death on a cross.
> Therefore God also highly exalted him
>   and gave him the name
>   that is above every name,
> so that at the name of Jesus
>   every knee should bend,
>   in heaven and on earth and under the earth,
> and every tongue should confess
>   that Jesus Christ is Lord,
>   to the glory of God the Father.
>
>   (Phil. 2:3–11)

Harry and Ron's attitude and actions of going down into the Chamber of Secrets to save Ginny, then being raised up can serve to remind us of Christ, who humbled himself to come down to save us, then was raised up from death and exalted to the heights of heaven. And Gilderoy Lockhart can remind us that everyone who exalts himself will be brought down.

A Songbird and an Old Hat

> *"This is what Dumbledore sends his defender! A songbird and an old hat! Do you feel brave, Harry Potter? Do you feel safe now?"*
>
> —Tom Riddle to Harry, Book Two, p. 316

When Fawkes, Dumbledore's pet phoenix, showed up piping its weird music, Tom Riddle knew Dumbledore was behind it. He laughed at Harry as the bird dropped the Sorting Hat at Harry's feet. Even Harry did not quite see how these could help him in a duel with Tom Riddle—especially without his wand, which Tom still held. But as things progressed, it turned out that these unlikely things were precisely what Harry needed.

Previously, when Harry had been alone in Professor Dumbledore's office with Fawkes, the sickly looking bird suddenly burst into flames. He watched in amazement as it was reborn out of the ashes. Dumbledore explained that this was the nature of phoenixes, their other fascinating characteristics being that they "can carry immensely heavy loads, their tears have healing powers, and they make highly *faithful* pets" (Book Two, p. 207).

Consider the characteristics of Professor Dumbledore's pet phoenix. Each of these can be related to the gospel. Its ability to rise from the ashes can be seen as symbolic of the promise of resurrection. Fawkes was the one who pecked out the basilisk's eyes, thereby destroying its murderous gaze. The ability of the phoenix to carry heavy loads served to lift up all who would hold on and carried them out of the Chamber, where Tom Riddle and the basilisk did their best to kill Harry. The tears the phoenix shed as

76

Harry lay dying showed compassion. The same tears also brought healing from the poisonous venom of the King of Snakes. If it had not been for the healing tears of the phoenix, Harry's wound would surely have been fatal.

As for the other item Dumbledore provided for Harry, the Sorting Hat declared which house each student at Hogwarts would be in. Although the Sorting Hat had considered putting Harry in Slytherin, and said he could have been great there, it had openly declared Harry to be a Gryffindor. In his showdown with Tom Riddle, Harry needed to have confidence that he *belonged* in Gryffindor while fighting against evil. The battle this time was partly in the form of Tom Riddle playing with Harry's mind by suggesting that they had a lot in common. Perhaps this was an attempt to keep Harry from fighting against him by undermining his confidence about belonging in Gryffindor. The Sorting Hat reminded Harry that he was a Gryffindor, and later supplied proof when he was able to pull the sword of Godric Gryffindor out of the hat.

How do a songbird and an old hat relate to the gospel? First, let's consider the symbolism of the phoenix. An Old Testament prophecy says, "But for you who revere my name the sun of righteousness shall rise, with healing in its wings. You shall go out leaping like calves from the stall. And you shall tread down the wicked, for they will be ashes under the soles of your feet, on the day when I act, says the LORD of hosts" (Mal. 4:2–3). Here we see the imagery of a bird with healing powers rising up to help the righteous triumph over the wicked. Most commentaries consider this a messianic prophecy. Although no use is made directly in the New Testament of the exact phrases "sun of righteousness" or "healing in his wings," there is an image of the glorified Son of Man (Jesus) in which his face is described like "the sun shining with full force" with a two-edged sword coming from his mouth (Rev. 1:16).

Consider these parallels: Jesus was sent by the Father, and was *faithful* to his mission. He was so faithful that when he struggled in prayer on the night he was to be betrayed, he was able to say, "Father, if you are willing, remove this cup from me"—referring to the cup of God's wrath and the suffering that awaited him on the cross—"yet, not my will but yours be done" (Luke 22:42).

Jesus offers to carry our heavy burdens: "Come to me, all you that are weary and are carrying heavy burdens, and I will give you rest" (Matt. 11:28). What are these heavy burdens that the Messiah would bear for us? Christians cherish the prophecy found in Isaiah:

> Surely he has borne our infirmities
>   and carried our diseases;
> yet we accounted him stricken,
>   struck down by God, and afflicted.
> But he was wounded for our transgressions,
>   crushed for our iniquities;
> upon him was the punishment that made us whole,
>   and by his bruises we are healed.
>
> (Isa. 53:4–5)

Since Jesus carried these burdens, he has compassion for us. He was a man of sorrows and acquainted with grief. He wept at the grave of his friend, Lazarus, even though he knew that moments later he would raise him back to life. The phoenix wept at Harry's side when Tom Riddle enjoyed watching him die: "'You're dead, Harry Potter,' said Riddle's voice above him. 'Dead. Even Dumbledore's bird knows it. Do you see what he's doing, Potter? He's crying.'" Harry was dying from the basilisk's deadly venom, but his death was interrupted and reversed by the ministry of the phoenix. Similarly, the Bible says, "And you were dead in your trespasses and sins" (Eph. 2:1 NASB), but Christ came to interrupt and reverse death to give us new life. The bird's tears healed Harry of the fatal wound. Likewise, the one who has died and rose again himself has the power to heal us from the fatal venom of sin and raise us back to eternal life.

With regard to the Sorting Hat, does the Bible speak of a head covering that can assure us that we belong in a house other than the one ruled by the evil one? The apostle Paul declares, "For our struggle is not against enemies of blood and flesh, but against the rulers, against the authorities, against the cosmic powers of this present darkness, against the spiritual forces of evil in the heavenly places. Therefore take up the whole armor of God, so that you may be able to withstand on that evil day, and having done everything, to stand firm" (Eph. 6:12–13). This passage goes on to describe the full armor of God, which includes a head covering: the helmet of salvation. Like Harry we need to *know* we are saved in order to have courage for the battles with the evil one.

The Sorting Hat that was handed to Harry during his battle reminded him that he had been chosen to be in Gryffindor. God wants his children to remember that they were securely placed in Christ by the Holy Spirit. Therefore, we can confidently resist the accusations of the enemy when he tries to undermine our confident faith. It is from such assurance of mind that the Christian can draw the "sword of the Spirit," which is the word of God to defeat the evil one while engaged in spiritual battles. So the weapons Dumbledore sent Harry were formidable indeed, as are the ones provided to those in Christ.

The Rescue of Ginny Weasley

"Ginny, please wake up," Harry muttered desperately,
shaking her. Ginny's head lolled hopelessly from side to
side.
"She won't wake," said a soft voice.

Book Two, p. 307

As improbable as it seemed, Ginny Weasley was the guilty one. She had trusted herself to Tom Riddle, who reached her through his enchanted diary. Progressively she poured herself into that diary, and Tom Riddle poured himself back into her. She was soon following the course he set out for her. He became her ruler, causing her to do terrible things. She was the one killing Hagrid's roosters to protect the basilisk. She had loosed the monstrous snake on the school. In the end, she was taken captive by Tom Riddle to lure Harry down into the Chamber of Secrets. This left Ginny as good as dead, under the control of one whose nature was murderous.

Then Harry arrived, killed the basilisk, defeated Tom Riddle, and sent him back where he came from. When Tom Riddle's memory was destroyed by the venom of his own snake, Ginny's life came streaming back into her. Then Fawkes raised them all up through the pipes and guided them to Professor McGonagall's office. There they were greeted with loving embraces. The whole story came out, even the troublesome truth that Ginny had been enchanted by Voldemort himself and that she was guilty.

Ginny was terribly afraid she would be expelled. After all, that was what happened to Hagrid, the last person thought to have opened the Chamber of Secrets. And he had been framed, while Ginny actually did the deeds. However, Dumbledore waived the punishment and sent her to Madam Pomfrey in the hospital wing with a prescription for hot chocolate. Ginny had not done anything to deserve such favor. She deserved to be expelled, maybe worse. But Headmaster Dumbledore extended his gracious kindness to her.

This sequence of events can be likened to a retrospective of what happens to those who put their faith in Christ for salvation. The Letter to the Ephesians says, "You were dead through the trespasses and sins in which you once lived, following the course of this world, following the ruler of the power of the air, the spirit that is now at work among those who are disobedient" (Eph. 2:1–2).

Even though few of us have done something as destructive as to loose the king of snakes on our classmates, "All of us once lived among [those who are disobedient] in the passions of our flesh, following the desires of flesh and senses, and we were by nature children of wrath, like everyone else. But God, who is rich in mercy, out of the great love with which he loved us even when we were dead through our trespasses, made us alive together with Christ" (Eph. 2:3–5). We were not physically dead, but as long as we were without rescue, under the control of the evil one, we were as good as dead and sure to end up dead if Christ had not rescued us, apart from anything we could have done to save ourselves.

The Bible goes on to explain, "[God] raised us up with him and seated us with him in the heavenly places in Christ Jesus, so that in the ages to come he might show the immeasurable riches of his grace in kindness toward us in Christ Jesus" (Eph. 2:6–7). When the King of Snakes was defeated, Ginny came back to life. Similarly, Christ's death on the cross destroyed the "snake" that strikes with the venom of sin that brings death. Christ took the venom of sin and death for us. He died and conquered death for us. All who put their trust in Christ are raised up with him. Satan has not been utterly destroyed yet, just as Tom Riddle's memory only went away, to rise again another time. The good news of the gospel includes God's firm assurance that the snake (Satan) will ultimately be defeated and cast into hell forever, never to torment anyone ever again for all eternity. We are just not to that part of our story yet.

The Bible describes all of this as a work of grace: "For by grace you have been saved through faith, and this is not your own doing; it is the gift of God—not the result of works, so that no one may boast" (Eph. 2:8–9). What is this grace? Unmerited favor on top of mercy. It would have been mercy if Dumbledore simply did not punish Ginny as she deserved. God's goodness toward us includes mercy, not receiving the punishment we deserve, but also grace, receiving the favor we know we do not deserve. As Ginny was treated with such love and kindness by Dumbledore after she was rescued, so too God will treat all who are saved. As we think of how Ginny headed toward the hospital wing, looking forward to a steaming mug of hot chocolate instead of packing her bags, she can represent a small taste of what the grace of God is like.

Dumbledore's Remedy for Doubt

"Only a true Gryffindor could have pulled that *out of the hat, Harry."*
—Dumbledore to Harry, Book Two, p. 334

After Harry survived his battle with Tom Riddle and the basilisk, he was still deeply disturbed by some things Tom Riddle suggested to him about their apparent similarities. Dumbledore did not deny these, including a "certain disregard for rules," but reminded Harry that the Sorting Hat had put him in Gryffindor even though it could see the similarities that Tom Riddle pointed out. Dumbledore had a remedy for Harry's doubt. His proof that Harry belonged in Gryffindor was to point him to the blood-stained silver sword, with the name of Godric Gryffindor engraved above the hilt.

Harry had been declared to be *in Gryffindor* when the Sorting Hat sorted him. Those who trust Christ are declared to be *in Christ*. The Bible explains that we have been *chosen* to be *in Christ*. This is not something earned, but declared. Harry's place in Gryffindor was not based on him being perfectly good. Likewise, our security in Christ is not based on our being perfectly good, although we do want to please God who calls us to be holy (which could be compared to how Harry wants to please Dumbledore). Dumbledore put Harry's doubts to rest with assurance that he had the sword that proved he belonged in Gryffindor. It is being *in Christ* and relying on his righteousness that gives us confidence that we belong in

God's family and will remain accepted there. Even the apostle Paul had to come to grips with the fact that he sometimes did the very things he hated, and did not do the very good he sought to do. In light of recognizing this inner struggle with evil inclinations, Paul exclaims, "Wretched man that I am! Who will rescue me from this body of death? Thanks be to God through Jesus Christ our Lord!" (Rom. 7:24–25). His assurance that he is *in Christ* is key.

The gospel shows that it is not being perfectly good, without any sinful inclinations, that makes one right with God. Rather, it is knowing that even on our best day, with the best intentions, when we still struggle against evil externally and internally, our hope is found by being *in Christ*. Later in the same letter, Paul gives strong assurance to help Christians put doubts to rest: "For I am convinced that neither death, nor life, nor angels, nor rulers, nor things present, nor things to come, nor powers, nor height, nor depth, nor anything else in all creation, will be able to separate us from the love of God in Christ Jesus our Lord" (Rom. 8:38–39; see also 8:31–37).

Since the "sword of the Spirit" is the word of God, perhaps the passage above from God's word will give us a confidence similar to that which put Harry's doubts to rest when Dumbledore pointed him to the name engraved on the hilt of the sword of Godric Gryffindor.

Dobby's Sock and Other
Tales of Redemption

*"Got a sock," said Dobby in disbelief. "Master threw it,
and Dobby caught it, and Dobby—Dobby is free."*
—Book Two, p. 338

*I*n introducing himself to Harry, Dobby explained that he is a
house-elf and therefore bound to serve one house and one family
forever. Unfortunately for Dobby, the house he served was the
house of Malfoy. House-elves are slaves, without possessions. A
house-elf wears rags of some sort because the terms of his enslave-
ment declares that if anyone in his family gives him a piece of
clothing, he will be free. That is why Dobby was wearing a pillow-
case when he met Harry. Dobby explained that his master and family were careful not to even give him so much as an old sock, so as
to keep him enslaved.

Harry's triumph over the Dark Lord had given hope to the
house-elves:

> "Ah, if Harry Potter only knew!" Dobby groaned, more
> tears dripping onto his ragged pillowcase. "If he only knew
> what he means to us, to the lowly, the enslaved, we dregs
> of the magical world! . . . But mostly, sir, life has improved
> for my kind since you triumphed over He-Who-Must-Not-
> Be-Named. Harry Potter survived, and the Dark Lord's
> power was broken, and it was a new dawn, sir, and Harry
> Potter shone like a beacon of hope for those of us who
> thought the Dark days would never end, sir." (Book Two,
> pp. 177–78)

When Dobby met Harry it had been twelve years since Volde-mort's power was broken, but Dobby himself had not benefited much personally. He was still enslaved to a cruel master, Lucius Malfoy. When the whole story came out, we learned that Mr. Mal-foy played a key role in the dark deeds that happened at Hogwarts that year. He had slipped Tom Riddle's diary into Ginny's book. When Mr. Malfoy came storming into Hogwarts at the end of Book Two, Dobby was bobbing at his feet, still trying to polish his shoes. Dumbledore set Mr. Malfoy straight by letting him know that he was back in power and knew what Mr. Malfoy had done. As Mr. Malfoy stormed out, kicking Dobby down the hall, Harry had a great idea.

Harry tricked Mr. Malfoy into tossing Dobby his old sock. Once Dobby caught the sock, he realized that he was free. Mr. Malfoy was furious that his unwitting gift of a garment had cost him his slave, but there was nothing he could do. Dobby was free, and once free, he could use his considerable magical powers to protect him-self and others from Mr. Malfoy. So when Dobby said that Mr. Malfoy had to leave, Mr. Malfoy *had* to leave.

The house-elves saw Harry as a light in their darkness. He gave them hope that there was some way to break the power of the Dark Lord who ruled so cruelly. Likewise, the prophecies of a coming Jewish Messiah were a light of hope even to non-Jewish people. Indeed, the promised Messiah gave hope to all those who were oppressed and who longed for freedom from cruel masters. Long before Jesus was born, the Bible prophesied that the Messiah would be a light to the Gentiles, like a light dawning for people who sat in darkness (see Matt. 4:16). Jesus fulfilled the specific prophecies when he went to live in "Galilee of the Gentiles." Jesus came to those who had no claim on salvation. He did not come to call the righteous—or self-righteous—but those enslaved to sin. When Jesus died and rose again, he broke the curse and offered a new dawn of hope, not just to the Jews, but to all who would believe in him.

This sense that Jesus was the promised light in the darkness was reinforced by the prophecy John the Baptist's father gave about his son:

> And you, child, will be called the prophet of the Most High;
>   for you will go before the Lord to prepare his ways,
> to give knowledge of salvation to his people
>   by the forgiveness of their sins.
> By the tender mercy of our God,
>   the dawn from on high will break upon us,
> to give light to those who sit in darkness and in the shadow
>   of death,
>   to guide our feet into the way of peace.
>   (Luke 1:76–79)

When Jesus began his public ministry, he came to the synagoguc in his home town of Nazareth. He publicly read a familiar passage from the prophet Isaiah. This passage was commonly understood as a prediction of what the awaited messiah would do. Jesus astounded the audiencc by announcing that this prophecy had been fulfilled that day, in their hearing. Here is what Jesus read:

> The Spirit of the Lord is upon me,
>   because he has anointed me to bring good news to the poor.
> He has sent me to proclaim release to the captives
>   and recovery of sight to the blind,
>   to let the oppressed go free,
> to proclaim the year of the Lord's favor.
>   (Luke 4:18–19, reading from Isa. 61:1–2)

This "year of the Lord's favor" refers to the Year of Jubilee, when once each fiftieth year all the slaves in Israel were to be set free. Jesus declared himself to be the one who would release the captives and let the oppressed go free. This is backed up later in the Letter to the Galatians: "For freedom Christ has set us free. Stand firm, therefore, and do not submit again to a yoke of slavery" (Gal. 5:1). This theme carries on throughout the New Testament.

The Bible describes people as slaves to sin, under a malevolent master. Unless we are freed, we are destined to be slaves forever. We too are clothed in spiritual rags, because the Bible says that even our best efforts are like "filthy rags" when what we really need are "garments of salvation" and "robes of righteousness": "I will greatly rejoice in the LORD, my whole being shall exult in my God; for he has clothed me with the garments of salvation, he has covered me with the robe of righteousness" (Isa. 61:10).

Dobby's sock can be a symbol of redemption. The idea is that something is given as a ransom to buy back or purchase the freedom of something or someone held captive. When the payment is made, the captive can go free. Our "garments of salvation" come in the form of the righteous blood of Jesus Christ that he gave as a ransom to pay our debt of sin. Therefore, "You know that you were ransomed from the futile ways inherited from your ancestors, not with perishable things like silver or gold, but with the precious blood of Christ" (1 Pet. 1:18–19).

We cannot be freed until someone gives us these robes of righteousness. We cannot get our own righteousness, and our master certainly is not going to help us out. He wants us to stay enslaved to him. The robes of righteousness have been purchased for us by Christ. In effect, they were tossed to us—unwittingly—by those acting under Satan's influence who put Jesus to death. They thought they were just killing him, when really they were acting to deliver the redemption God wanted us to receive.

Even though Christ came a long time ago, many individuals have not personally experienced the freedom he came to bring. Jesus has purchased the "garments of salvation" for us; he offers us his own righteousness in exchange for our old rags of our best efforts. But we have to take hold of it for ourselves, like Dobby catching that sock that set him free. Now that this garment has been offered, we each have to lay hold of it by faith. Then we can exclaim, as Dobby did, "I am free! I am free!"

Once we are freed by Christ, our obligation to live as slaves to sin and in Satan's control is over. Thereafter, we are commanded to be careful not to submit again to such slavery. We are given the power of the Holy Spirit so that we can resist our old master's attempts to enslave us again. We would do well to behave like Dobby and send our old master packing.

Glimmers of the Gospel in Book Three

Harry Potter and the Prisoner of Azkaban

Introduction to Book Three

*I*n Book Three we see the tenacious struggle required to bring about justice in a world fraught with injustice. Sirius Black had been wrongly accused, convicted, and imprisoned for more than a decade for a crime he did not commit, while the guilty one went free. Buckbeak the Hippogriff was unjustly condemned to death on the false accusations of one who gave and garnered false testimony. In Book Two, Hagrid was imprisoned unjustly because of the cloud of suspicion that remained over him based on a false accusation and conviction for something he had not done. He had been wrongfully expelled from Hogwarts because he had been framed for opening the Chamber of Secrets fifty years earlier, although he had not done so.

To counter these acts and effects of injustice, Dumbledore allows Harry, Ron, and Hermione to uncover the truth, which helps to correct some of the effects of injustice. Harry and Hermione are commissioned to do what they can to save innocent lives, and at least free them from the ultimate infliction of unjust punishments until the injustice can be overcome with true justice.

A secondary theme of Book Three is learning to find ways to overcome our fears and painful memories of the worst times of our lives rather than to give in to despair or fear. This is addressed by learning to counteract the power of the boggarts and the dementors. We also see a corollary in the life of Professor Lupin, who does not let the personal challenges associated with being a werewolf keep him from trying his best to be a productive member of society. We see that he is poor, probably because it is hard for a werewolf to find work in the wizarding world, but he still risks misunderstanding and criticism in order to contribute by teaching Defense Against the Dark Arts.

In the Company of Albus Dumbledore

> *Harry happened to agree wholeheartedly with Mrs. Weasley that the safest place on earth was wherever Albus Dumbledore happened to be.*
>
> —Book Three, p. 67

Albus Dumbledore, Headmaster of Hogwarts, is a somewhat mysterious character. The reader gets the impression that there is far more to him than anyone yet knows. However, we do know that Dumbledore engenders trust among those on the side of good, making them feel safer for being in his presence. In his first year, when Harry knows someone is trying to hurt or kill him, he is tremendously relieved to see Professor Dumbledore in the stands for the Quidditch match. And Dumbledore makes evildoers think twice before doing anything amiss while he is around.

Here is some of what we know so far: Dumbledore was the Transfiguration teacher fifty years earlier, when Tom Riddle was a student. When Tom framed Hagrid for opening the Chamber of Secrets, Dumbledore was the only one who was not fooled. He kept a close watch on Tom thereafter, so it was not safe for him to open the Chamber again. He is one of the few people unafraid to call Voldemort by name. When Harry's parents were murdered, Dumbledore decided Harry would be better off living with his Muggle aunt and uncle and delivered him to their doorstep personally. Dumbledore gave Harry the Invisibility Cloak his father left him, and permission to be on the Gryffindor Quidditch team his first year. Dumbledore is famous for his defeat of the dark wizard Grindelwald in 1945. He doesn't need an Invisibility Cloak to become invisible. He made sure Harry found the Mirror of Erised, understood how it worked, and was prepared if he should ever run across it again. We later learn that Dumbledore had hidden the Sorcerer's Stone in the mirror. The knowledge Dumbledore arranged for Harry to learn is what helped him defeat Quirrell and Voldemort. In Harry's second year, again it was Dumbledore who gave Harry the knowledge he needed to prepare for his battle with Tom Riddle (aka: You-Know-Who), by explaining that his presence would be available to anyone who remained loyal to him and that help would come to anyone at Hogwarts who asked for it. In the battle, Harry's survival and victory hinged on his loyalty to Dumbledore. And it was the weapons Dumbledore sent that Harry used to defeat the basilisk and Tom Riddle.

When injustice is in the works, Dumbledore manages to help set things right—as right as things can be while people are either too afraid to stand up to evil or unable to see the truth. He made sure Sirius and Buckbeak escaped, and that Hagrid was released from Azkaban. He gave Hagrid a teaching post once his name was cleared of the crime Tom Riddle framed him for. (This took fifty years, but it seems that Dumbledore is extremely patient or has a different view of time than most.)

While Dumbledore is staunchly on the side of good, and tremendously powerful, he often stands back to let those on the good side take up the battle (providing overarching security, guidance, weapons, and instruction). When Hermione and Harry told him the truth about Peter Pettigrew and asked if he believed them, he answered, "Yes, I do. . . . But I have no power to make other men see the truth, or to overrule the Minister of Magic." Instead of providing the solution for them, Dumbledore pointed the way for them to bring about justice and help save innocent lives. While it seems that he could set everything right in an instant, he allows the battle to play out and helps those looking up to him to engage in the battle themselves.

Dumbledore seems unusually open to giving people second chances, and redeeming those who have been rejected in wizarding society: He hired Professor Lupin even though he knew he was a werewolf. When Hagrid was expelled, he arranged for Headmaster

Dippet to keep him at Hogwarts and train him as Keeper of Keys. Dumbledore lets students attend Hogwarts without discriminating on the basis of their bloodline and magical heritage. Dumbledore never endorses breaking the rules, but exercises authority at Hogwarts in the form of humane punishments. He also exercises his prerogative to show mercy, forbearance, and grace to those caught breaking the rules.

While Dumbledore's power is greater than Voldemort's, he refuses to resort to the Dark Arts. Dumbledore is Ron's hero. Hagrid repeatedly calls him a great man, and will not tolerate anyone speaking against him. His staff respects him. The dementors fear him. When Harry and friends are really in trouble, they run to Dumbledore. As Harry realized his first year, Dumbledore seems to know everything that is going on, but holds back to let his students fight the battles. Then he shows up afterward, to give some insight and provide lessons. His provision of safety does not preclude casualties—which do occur when evil is on the loose—but Dumbledore is actively engaged in the fight against evil.

We also see that Dumbledore presents a danger for those on the side of evil. When Professor Quirrell admitted that he had tried to knock Harry off his broom, he also said that Snape's countercurse was unnecessary since he could not have done anything to harm Harry with Dumbledore watching. Before Harry and friends went down the trapdoor, someone lured Dumbledore away (presumably because that would remove a measure of protection for those on the good side). Lucius Malfoy did all in his power to have Dumbledore removed as Headmaster, but when Dumbledore bested him, Malfoy dared not challenge him directly. Tom Riddle admitted that he could not let the monster out of the Chamber of Secrets again while he was a student at Hogwarts because of Dumbledore. He had to preserve his memory in the diary, hoping for a time when Dumbledore would be less of a threat to his evil plans. As it turned out, that was not the case.

Dumbledore's attitude is typically cheerful, kind, long-suffering, calm, and there is usually a twinkle in his eye. However, when faced with an assault of evil, he is strong and unyielding. He is compassionate toward those who are weak or who have fallen under the influence of the evil one, but he does not interfere with the consequences they bring upon themselves if they have willingly conspired to do evil. When someone such as Ginny Weasley is overtaken by evil unwittingly or against her will, he does not punish severely, but corrects. Overall, Dumbledore seems to genuinely love people. He stands staunchly on the side of good, but hates evil, even while showing compassion for those destroyed by the evil they embrace.

Hmmm . . . Perhaps you can draw your own parallels here.

Let the Feast Begin!

> *"Let the feast begin!" [said Dumbledore.]*
> *The golden plates and goblets before them filled suddenly*
>   *with food and drink.*
>
> —Book Three, pp. 93–94

*O*ne of the most marvelous and enjoyable aspects of life at Hogwarts is the magical meals. It is great fun for the students to sit down at a table and to watch all their favorite foods appear—especially for Harry, who had never been allowed to eat enough to really satisfy his hunger: "The Dursleys had never exactly starved Harry, but he'd never been allowed to eat as much as he liked" (Book One, p. 123). The feasts were especially lavish, but every day, at every meal, the food magically appeared on their plates in the Great Hall. Then, when the meal was over the plates were magically clean again. (Of course, we later learn that even such magic requires the service of willing house-elves working in the kitchens.)

When Jesus went about teaching people about the kingdom of God, he attracted massive crowds because of the miracles he was performing, mostly healing the sick and casting demons out of people tormented by them. Kurt Bruner, author of *Finding God in the Lord of the Rings,* pointed out in a radio interview that the use of good magic in fantasy stories could be compared to that which is miraculous in the real world. Some people who saw the miracles of Jesus may have thought of him as a magician.

Jesus was far more than a magician, however. He would soon make this clear to the gathering crowd by the message that accompanied his miraculous signs. This complimentary meal would be followed by an after-dinner talk they would never forget. The miracle Jesus was about to perform would speak a language everyone understands: hunger satisfaction.

John 6:1–13 tells the familiar story about Jesus feeding the crowd by the Sea of Galilee: "One of his disciples, Andrew, Simon Peter's brother, said to him, 'There is a boy here who has five barley loaves and two fish. But what are they among so many people?'" (John 6:8–9). Notice here that Jesus let a small but willing servant help deliver up the miracle meal, not unlike what Dumbledore did by employing the house-elves in his kitchens. "Then Jesus took the loaves, and when he had given thanks, he distributed them to those who were seated; so also the fish, *as much as they wanted*. When they were satisfied, he told his disciples, 'Gather up the fragments left over, so that nothing may be lost.' So they gathered them up, and from the fragments of the five barley loaves, left by those who had eaten, they filled twelve baskets" (John 6:11–13).

As at Hogwarts, this was an all-you-can-eat meal and cleanup was provided! But Jesus was not just doing tricks with fish and bread, nor was he only concerned with his audience's physical hunger. He was aiming to teach the people a vital spiritual truth. This crowd was expecting a prophet to arise to free them from the oppressive Roman government under which they lived. Moses had promised the people of Israel, "The LORD your God will raise up for you a prophet like me from among your own brothers. You must listen to him" (Deut. 18:15 NIV). They remembered how Moses was good at serving up regular meals and were now wondering if Jesus could be the one Moses told them to expect.

"When the people saw the sign that he had done, they began to say, 'This is indeed the prophet who is to come into the world'" (John 6:14). A political action committee formed right then and there. Someone came to the conclusion that they should make Jesus their king and have him fulfill all the other prophecies the Messiah would fulfill. They especially liked the part about their enemies being overthrown. John continues, "When Jesus realized that they were about to come and take him by force to make him king, he withdrew again to the mountain by himself" (John 6:15).

What's the point? These people were focused on earthly food and political power. Jesus went on to explain, "Do not work for the food that perishes, but for the food that endures for eternal life, which the Son of Man will give you. For it is on him that God the Father has set his seal" (John 6:27).

But the people still did not understand; they were seeking bread to satisfy a mere physical hunger. Jesus put it to them this way: "I am the bread of life. *Whoever comes to me will never be hungry, and whoever believes in me will never be thirsty*" (John 6:35).

Jesus used a "magical meal" to get their attention and then to aim it at the deeper hunger of the soul. The Bible is replete with imagery and events that relate to satisfying our hunger. The promises of heaven include a banquet where Jesus will once again sit with his disciples, to eat and drink. Psalm 23 looks forward to a time when God will prepare a banquet for us in the presence of our enemies. All of this correlates our experience of never quite getting enough, knowing recurrent hunger, and ultimately receiving the satisfaction available through that which God has provided. On a spiritual level, Jesus declared that he is the "true bread" that alone can satisfy the hunger of our souls.

But Jesus was not avoiding the practical need of people—he was getting first things first. He would teach those who became his disciples to pray to the Father for all they would need in body and soul. That prayer includes this provision: "Give us this day our daily bread" (Matt. 6:11). So when we enjoy reading about the magical meals at Hogwarts and seeing Harry finally be satisfied, let us remember that God wants nothing less for us.

Grim Omens of Death
Prove Misleading

> *"The Grim, my dear, the Grim!" cried Professor Trelawney. . . . "My dear boy, it is an omen—the worst omen—of death!"*
> —Madam Trelawney to Harry, Book Three, p. 107

*I*t was a bit unsettling for Harry to start his third year at Hogwarts the way he did. After losing his temper, blowing up Aunt Marge, and running away, he was rescued by the Knight Bus and taken to the Leaky Cauldron. There he overheard that an escaped prisoner was probably on his way to try to murder him. Harry was troubled by his own conscience, but also by the sighting of a giant black dog, which he learned could be called "the Grim." According to his rather odd divination teacher, Professor Sibyll Trelawney, the Grim is the giant, spectral dog that haunts churchyards and is an omen of death.

No wonder Harry did not want to tell anyone about the black dog he had seen the night he ran away. Harry had looked it up in a book called *Death Omens: What to Do When You Know the Worst Is Coming,* but that had not helped. The bookshop manager had tried to turn him to other interests, saying, "Oh, I wouldn't read that if I were you. . . . You'll start seeing death omens everywhere. It's enough to frighten anyone to death" (Book Three, p. 54). When Professor Trelawney claimed to have seen the Grim in Harry's teacup on the first day of class, the implications were truly upsetting.

Professor McGonagall tried to set her students straight: "You should know, Potter, that Sibyll Trelawney has predicted the death of one student a year since she arrived at this school. None of them has died yet. Seeing death omens is her favorite way of greeting a new class. If it were not for the fact that I never speak ill of my colleagues—" (Book Three, p. 109).

Even though Madam Trelawney's belief in death omens is belittled by a more sensible professor, Harry still endures much worry under the shadow of his own superstitions. Then it turned out that the black dog he saw was not the Grim at all; it was really someone who cared for him very much, in the form of an Animagus. Harry's belief in omens misled him, and caused him much unnecessary worry.

The Bible has this to say about those who believe in omens:

> Thus says the LORD, your Redeemer,
>   who formed you in the womb:
> I am the LORD, who made all things,
>   who alone stretched out the heavens,
>   who by myself spread out the earth;
> who frustrates the omens of liars,
>   and makes fools of diviners;
> who turns back the wise
>   and makes their knowledge foolish;
> who confirms the word of his servant
>   and fulfills the prediction of his messengers.
>   (Isa. 44:24–26a)

This certainly seems to have something to say in reference to Professor Trelawney.

The Bible tells us not to look to omens; rather, we are to look to and trust the predictions of God's messengers recorded in the Bible. Jesus also directly warned against false prophets who would come producing signs and omens, with the result of leading people astray. Jesus said this in regard to the time of his own return:

> For false messiahs and false prophets will appear and produce great signs and omens, to lead astray, if possible, even

the elect. Take note, I have told you beforehand. So, if they say to you, "Look! He is in the wilderness," do not go out. If they say, "Look! He is in the inner rooms," do not believe it. For as the lightning comes from the east and flashes as far as the west, so will be the coming of the Son of Man. (Matt. 24:24–27)

The omen of death Harry thought he saw was really in his mind, which had been filled with superstitious fears. These proved to be unfounded and counterproductive. Instead of looking for omens, Jesus said we should be looking for the signs of his coming, which will not be nearly as obscure or open for speculation as an omen.

One might wonder why Dumbledore would leave Professor Trelawney in her position when he makes clear to Harry that he knew she did not give accurate predictions, and that she may have even been the mouthpiece for a prophecy that Voldemort's servant would return to him and aid in his return to power. Does this have any biblical parallel? Indeed it does. It is an explanation for why questionable characters are allowed to remain in the ranks of those who claim to be representatives of God's kingdom.

Jesus told this parable:

The kingdom of heaven may be compared to someone who sowed good seed in his field; but while everybody was asleep, an enemy came and sowed weeds among the wheat, and then went away. So when the plants came up and bore grain, then the weeds appeared as well. And the slaves of the householder came and said to him, "Master, did you not sow good seed in your field? Where, then, did these weeds come from?" He answered, "An enemy has done this." The slaves said to him, "Then do you want us to go and gather them?" But he replied, "No; for in gathering the weeds you would uproot the wheat along with them. Let both of them grow together until the harvest; and at harvest time I will tell the reapers, Collect the weeds first and bind them in bundles to be burned, but gather the wheat into my barn." (Matt. 13:24–30)

This seems to parallel Dumbledore's policy with regard to his staff. As is true throughout the Harry Potter books, it is not always easy to tell who is truly on the side of good or evil. If those who presumed some were evil and had eliminated them when they had the chance (Sirius Black comes to mind), tragedy would have occurred. Likewise, one cannot trust that those who claim to be on the side of good truly are (think of Professor Quirrell and Gilderoy Lockhart). In these stories, and in life, we must always remain on the alert and recognize that just because someone claims to be on the "good" side, it does not mean he or she truly is. By their deeds we will know them: A true prophet is known by an accuracy rate of 100 percent. Apparently we can expect some weeds to grow up with the good seed.

Judging from Professor Trelawney's dismal track record with her predictions and recurrent sightings of the death omen, one might suspect that she will turn out to be a weed. However, there is much we cannot know until the story is fully told, both in the Harry Potter books and in human history.

The good news here is that Madam Trelawney's death omen for Harry proved misleading. Instead of an omen of death, the giant black dog turned out to be a watch dog looking to protect Harry. He did not have to fear death because someone—his godfather—was watching over him to protect him all along. So too for those who put their trust in their God-Father in heaven rather than superstitions.

Fred and George and Original Sin

"Well . . . when we were in our first year, Harry—young,
*   carefree, and innocent—"*
Harry snorted. He doubted whether Fred and George had
*   ever been innocent.*

—Book Three, p. 191

*F*red and George Weasley are confirmed mischief makers, albeit good-hearted and fun-loving ones. Innocent? No! No one would ever buy that line. Fred and George continually get in trouble for sneaking out, swiping food from the kitchens, and pulling off practical jokes like when they left Ton-Tongue Toffees where Dudley was sure to find them. When they bequeathed their prized possession—the Marauder's Map—to Harry, it was intended as a supreme act of goodwill. However, Fred and George explained that in order to use the map the user had to say, "I solemnly swear that I am up to no good."

It is easy to see through Fred and George's claims of innocence, but not so easy with other characters who put more stock in being good and keeping the laws of the wizarding world. Hermione Granger could rightly be characterized as the conscience of her group, often dissuading them from wrongdoing. Mr. Weasley works in law enforcement for the Ministry of Magic. And yet, even these characters who aim to keep the law end up sometimes breaking the rules and laws they seemed so committed to uphold.

Hermione never stops being keenly aware of what is right, and feels deep pangs of conscience when she breaks the rules; however, she does break them at times. Mr. Weasley, who patrols others to make sure they are not misusing Muggle artifacts, cannot resist doing so himself. The flying car he rigged up secretly in his garage got Harry and Ron to school their second year, but also got them—and Mr. Weasley—into a lot of trouble. So, Fred, George, Hermione, Mr. Weasley, and all the "good" characters share a troubling flaw in common even with the Slytherins (except that Slytherins seem to be lacking pangs of conscience).

Many Christians would explain such universal inclinations toward wrongdoing—whether occasional or chronic—with the doctrine of original sin. The Bible makes it clear that every person is born a sinner, and comes from a long line of sinners dating all the way back to the first man and woman God created. They were created with free will, but when they chose to disobey God, a compulsion toward disobedience became inherent in human nature. The only exception to this in those born of a woman was Jesus Christ, the only begotten Son of God, conceived of the Holy Spirit.

This realization that even the best of the "good" characters are not constantly good may be disturbing to some. It reminds me of a line from the animated sitcom *The Simpsons,* when Homer buys a Bible at a yard sale. After flipping through it, he remarks, "Talk about a preachy book! Everybody in here is a sinner, except this guy"—presumably referring to Jesus.

This realization that "everybody in here is a sinner"—even those who try their very best to be good, and some like Fred and George who don't try as hard as others—is a necessary realization before one can go on to find the remedy for sin. In short, the gospel cannot be good news until you realize the bad news that you too are a sinner in need of a Savior. While such a realization may be troubling to folks like Hermione, this is a fundamental teaching of the Bible: "There is no one who is righteousness, not even one" (Rom. 3:10).

The Bible upholds a supremely high absolute moral standard, but being able to live according to that moral standard requires the help of God's Holy Spirit. As in the Harry Potter stories, Bible characters run the gamut between those who stay well within God's moral law most of the time with only occasional lapses, those who seem to make a career of breaking the rules (Jacob comes to mind) then have a dramatic turnaround, or those like Saul of Tarsus (who became Paul the apostle) who strictly followed God's law and were stunned to learn they were sinners like the rest.

The characters God singles out as heroes of the faith are listed in Hebrews 11, which is sometimes called the faith hall of fame. If we read this list in order to see if these are people who always did the right thing, we discover a wide range of sins in their lives. Everybody on that list was a sinner.

Fred and George could be seen as poster boys for the doctrine of original sin, but so too could all the other characters. Considering this can be instructive as we reflect on the sinful human condition. So when the Bible says, "All have sinned and fall short of the glory of God" (Rom. 3:23), we won't count ourselves out. This is good, because that leaves us open to be justified—not by our own presumed goodness but by God's grace received as a gift that comes through Jesus Christ (see Rom. 3:24). In understanding this, we can each come to agree with the apostle Paul: "The saying is sure and worthy of full acceptance, that Christ Jesus came into the world to save sinners—of whom I am the foremost" (1 Tim. 1:15).

Understanding that even the Hermiones and Mr. Weasleys of our world cannot be completely righteous can make those who identify more with Fred and George breathe a bit easier. It also paves the way to receive the good news that God loves all of us sinners and has a remedy for our sinful nature that cannot be achieved by keeping external laws alone.

The Department of Mysteries

"You've got to listen to me," Black said, and there was a note of urgency in his voice now. "You'll regret it if you don't. . . . You don't understand. . . ."
—Sirius Black to Harry, Book Three, p. 342

*T*hroughout the Harry Potter books it becomes apparent that the characters often think they have everything figured out, and they do—they have figured it out wrong. They see clues, they see suspicious behavior, they may see what they think is an omen or something incriminating about a particular character, but when the story unfolds they discover they had it all wrong. They did in fact see what they thought they saw, but they did not see it clearly: like when Hermione saw Snape muttering while looking up at Harry and his bucking broomstick in Book One and assumed Snape was jinxing it. It turned out that Professor Quirrell was the one trying to knock Harry off his broom, while Professor Snape was trying to protect him. Throughout the story, these characters' assumptions led to wrong conclusions, and sometimes wrong treatment of those whom they misunderstood.

Book Three is filled with suspense because what people believe, and sincerely think to be true, turns out to be very different from the truth. Indeed, if Harry had acted rashly on the basis of what he saw with his own eyes, what he believed on the basis of newspaper reports and the stories he heard from trusted friends, even adults he respected, he could have made terrible life-changing mistakes.

At one point, Mr. Weasley mentions that the Ministry of Magic has a Department of Mysteries, which handles things that are top secret. The Department of Mysteries could be a good description of how these stories unfold. Each one contains a mystery. Along with the characters, the reader begins to understand the importance of not being hasty in judgment because there is much that we may not see clearly. So we learn to reserve final judgment until we gain greater insight as the whole story unfolds.

According to the Bible, we should exercise that same caution in our own world and in the lives of the people with whom we have relationships. Paul wrote a letter to a church in the city of Corinth. These people had become Christians, but were having all kinds of problems with each other and in their worship practices. Paul goes over the problems they are having, addressing the specifics, but then he gets to the heart of his message, which is love: "Love is patient; love is kind; love is not envious or boastful or arrogant or rude. It does not insist on its own way; it is not irritable or resentful; it does not rejoice in wrongdoing, but rejoices in the truth. It bears all things, believes all things, hopes all things, endures all things. . . . Love never ends" (1 Cor. 13:4–8a).

Later on in the chapter he writes, "For now we see in a mirror, dimly, but then we will see face to face. Now I know only in part; then I will know fully, even as I have been fully known. And now faith, hope, and love abide, these three; and the greatest of these is love" (1 Cor. 13:12–13). Therefore, when we are not sure about someone, or even when we believe we have that person figured out, let's remember that we could be wrong, and pause before condemning someone. That is where the patience of love pays off.

God's good news really does come down to love. God loving us. Us loving God. Us loving each other with God's help. "In this is love, not that we loved God but that he loved us and sent his Son to be the atoning sacrifice for our sins. Beloved, since God loved us so much, we also ought to love one another. No one has ever seen God; if we love one another, God lives in us, and his love is perfected in us" (1 John 4:10–12).

Some people reject the Bible or the gospel because they don't have it all figured out. We are not going to have it all figured out or see everything clearly in this life. But we can see enough to respond to God's love.

The Rat Who Betrayed Harry's Parents

"You sold Lily and James to Voldemort," said Black, who
was shaking too. "Do you deny it?"
Peter Pettigrew burst into tears.
                                        —Book Three, p. 374

*R*on never suspected that his rat, Scabbers, was a rat in a far more significant way. It turns out that Scabbers was really Peter Pettigrew, who had gone to Hogwarts with Harry's father. Peter had been one of a band of friends that included James Potter, Remus Lupin, and Sirius Black. When Voldemort terrorized the wizarding world, James and Lily Potter stood against him. Their friends were all thought to be staunchly on the side of good, but it turned out there was a traitor in their midst.

James and Lily went into hiding in Godric Hollow with their baby, Harry. They depended on their friends to keep their whereabouts secret. By means of a Fidelius Charm, Voldemort would have been unable to find them as long as the friend they trusted as their Secret-Keeper kept their secret. They made Peter Pettigrew their Secret-Keeper, but he gave in to Lord Voldemort and betrayed them. His betrayal led directly to their deaths and to Voldemort's attack on Harry.

When Jesus lived on earth, he chose twelve disciples, whom he called his friends. One of them turned against him and betrayed him to the forces that had aligned themselves against him. Those who wanted to arrest and kill Jesus did not dare do it in daylight, for they feared the crowds who regarded Jesus as a prophet or as the Messiah. So they had to find out where he was staying at night. Judas, one of the twelve, went to those seeking to kill Jesus and offered to betray him. They paid him thirty pieces of silver. Then Judas went back to Jesus. He sat down to dinner with him for the Passover meal, where Jesus let him know that he was on to him. The Bible says that Satan entered into Judas and he went out. Later that night Judas went to the chief priests, who had assembled a military force to arrest Jesus. Judas led them to the Garden of Gethsemane, where Jesus had been praying. Judas gave the sign he had promised—the one whom he kissed was the one they should arrest: "While [Jesus] was still speaking, suddenly a crowd came, and the one called Judas, one of the twelve, was leading them. He approached Jesus to kiss him; but Jesus said to him, 'Judas, is it with a kiss that you are betraying the Son of Man?'" (Luke 22:47–48).

Sirius understood the demands of friendship and confronted Peter Pettigrew after forcing him to reveal himself (after he had been hiding as a rat for over a decade). Peter pleaded that he had given in to Voldemort because he was afraid the Dark Lord would have killed him. "'THEN YOU SHOULD HAVE DIED!' roared Black. 'DIED RATHER THAN BETRAY YOUR FRIENDS, AS WE WOULD HAVE DONE FOR YOU!'" (Book Three, p. 375).

We do not know whether James, Remus, and Sirius really would have died for their friend, but that is the ideal. Even Jesus upheld it: "No one has greater love than this, to lay down one's life for one's friends" (John 15:13). We do know that even though Jesus was betrayed by one of his friends, like James and Lily Potter he showed us the greatest act of love and friendship one can possibly demonstrate when he laid down his life for us.

Glimmers of the Gospel in Book Four

Harry Potter and the Goblet of Fire

Introduction to Book Four

Book Four's major theme is that the aggressive nature of evil must be aggressively resisted. One dare not ignore or try to pacify or appease the forces of evil; those who do so, do so to their own peril. The only way to deal with the forces of evil is to identify them, resist them, reveal their evil deeds, and aggressively seek to counteract their evil schemes. This is carried out by showing what Voldemort is setting out to do, the elaborate nature of his schemes, and that he thinks nothing of murdering the innocent once they are no longer useful to his aims. This is countered by Dumbledore's call for a parting of the ways and for all to declare which side they are on—good or evil—as the forces of good prepare to actively fight against evil with all their might.

Secondary themes include the following:

1. Those on the side of good must employ constant vigilance against an evil enemy who uses deception as a key tactic to accomplish evil aims. We see this primarily in the deception carried out by Barty Crouch Jr. in the guise of Mad-Eye Moody. The success of his ability to deceive the characters in the story as well as the readers is a powerful theme to reflect on when considering the message of the book.

2. The destructive influence of those who bear false witness is depicted in the character of Rita Skeeter. She continually twists the truth, generates gossip, and writes reports that include untrue statements along with half-truths and just enough facts to give her stories credibility. The destructive effects of false and misleading reports can be clearly seen throughout the story. We also see how

hard it is to counteract such destructive practices, but that it is good when this is done by those who are able to discover the truth, as Hermione did with Rita Skeeter.

3. The concern for social justice is also raised by Hermione's campaign to lift the house-elves up from their oppressive conditions. Her Society for the Promotion of Elf Welfare (S.P.E.W.) desires to help those less fortunate. This also acknowledges the challenges of helping those long enslaved to learn to function in a new way of life while treating them respectfully (as Albus Dumbledore did with Dobby and Winky).

4. Book Four ends with one of the most important themes summed up in this quote from Dumbledore: "Remember, if the time should come when you have to make a choice between what is right and what is easy, remember what happened to a boy who was good, and kind, and brave, because he strayed across the path of Lord Voldemort" (Book Four, p. 724). We are challenged to choose that which is right over that which is easy. When faced with such choices, we are called upon to remember the lost lives of innocent victims murdered by forces of evil, reminding ourselves that the forces of evil will justify any means to achieve their aims.

A Murderer from the Beginning

All the villagers cared about was the identity of their mur-
derer—for plainly, three apparently healthy people did
not all drop dead of natural causes on the same night.
                                        —Book Four, p. 2

*B*ook Four reveals Voldemort as a murderer from the beginning
of the story. He killed his own father and grandparents, partially
because his Muggle father abandoned his mother before he was
born. We already knew he had killed Harry's parents and many
others during his reign of terror when he was at his full power.
Book Four opens with the revelation that he also killed Brenda
Jorkins, and then recounts his murder of Frank Brice, who happened upon him hiding in the old Riddle House. Voldemort is still
plotting his return to power; his aims have not changed. The way
he terrorizes his own follower, Peter Pettigrew, shows his nature
has not changed either; only his form is diminished. The Dark Lord
cannot be dismissed. Thus, we see that the nature of evil is aggressive and must be stopped by force.

While some people may think of "sweet Jesus, meek and mild,"
the revelation of Jesus in the Bible shows that he was never soft
on evil. He recognized the nature of evil as murderous, and that
those who serve evil do their master's bidding—which is to hate,
murder, and destroy all that is good. Jesus certainly did not bow
to political correctness when he addressed his opponents. He

publicly told them, "You are from your father the devil, and you choose to do your father's desires. He was a murderer from the beginning and does not stand in the truth, because there is no truth in him" (John 8:44). Another time he said to them, "You snakes! You brood of vipers! How can you escape being sentenced to hell?" (Matt. 23:33).

Given that Voldemort has been shown to be devoted to the side of evil in these stories, we should not be surprised to find that he was a murderer from the beginning and that his followers will seek to carry out his murderous plans. In our world, when we see those who aggressively pursue and grasp for power by murderous means, we can rightly conclude that they are working on the side of evil and must be opposed outright.

Harry's Dreams Warn of Danger

"It was only a dream," said Ron bracingly. "Just a night-
mare."
"Yeah, but was it, though?" said Harry.
—Book Four, p. 149

Often in these stories Harry's sleep is disturbed by troubling dreams and pain in his scar. Sometimes these disturbances have come in the form of a warning that Voldemort was nearby. Sometimes, such as when the Death Eaters dared to attack Muggles at the Quidditch World Cup, Harry was awakened by danger happening nearby. In Book Four, Harry's dream—which Ron tried to convince him was just a nightmare—was a revelation of what the evil one was up to. It was a warning.

Throughout the Bible, God sometimes speaks to people by way of dreams. This does not mean that people should look to dreams as a means of knowing the future apart from God. Rather, we should take all our dreams, waking and sleeping, to God in prayer, understanding that dreams have been one way God has spoken in the past and that all impressions must be tested by God's word. In the Old Testament, Joseph had dreams that foretold his future rise to power in Egypt and his family bowing before him. The ability to interpret dreams was a gift God gave some, which was instrumental to God elevating them to positions of power, as was the case with Joseph (when he rightly interpreted the dreams of two of his

117

fellow prisoners and of Pharaoh) and Daniel (who was able to interpret the dream of the king of Babylon when none of the sorcerers, seers, astrologers, or magicians could).

God gave the following guidelines to Moses' brother, Aaron, and sister, Miriam: "When there are prophets among you, I the LORD make myself known to them in visions; I speak to them in dreams" (Num. 12:6). However, Deuteronomy 13:1–3 records a test that must be applied to check those who say their dreams have spiritual significance:

> If a prophet, or one who foretells by dreams, appears among you and announces to you a miraculous sign or wonder, and if the sign or wonder of which he has spoken takes place, and he says, "Let us follow other gods" (gods you have not known) "and let us worship them," you must not listen to the words of that prophet or dreamer. The LORD your God is testing you to find out whether you love him with all your heart and with all your soul. (NIV)

In our world, God makes it clear that there may be people who show real supernatural signs and dreams that really do come true, even if they do not speak for God. Therefore, the test God gives us centers on whether or not a person's aim is to direct people to God (who revealed himself in the Bible), and not to any other god.

The four Gospels record dramatic communication that took place through dreams and other supernatural means. The Messiah's coming was foretold in Old Testament prophecies that mention the virgin birth ("Therefore the Lord himself will give you a sign: The virgin will be with child and will give birth to a son, and will call him Immanuel"[Isa. 7:14 NIV]) and Mary having to go to Bethlehem where the Messiah had to be born ("But you, O Bethlehem of Ephrathah, who are one of the little clans of Judah, from you shall come forth for me one who is to rule in Israel, whose origin is from of old, from ancient days" [Mic. 5:2]). When these prophecies began to be fulfilled, the evil one did not just sit idle. The battle lines were drawn up and the forces of evil took action to try to stop God's prophecies from being fulfilled. Spiritual forces of evil, and people under their control, sought to kill the baby Jesus to try to keep him from growing up to fulfill the messianic prophecies.

In the birth narrative in Matthew 1:13–2:23, much of the communication from God comes through supernatural means: prophecies recorded in the Old Testament, signs in the heavens, and through dreams. Note the similarities between the battle of those on the side of evil versus those on the side of Jesus and the kind of battle we see unfold between good and evil in the Harry Potter stories.

When we see how the Harry Potter stories use dreams, prophecies, and signs in the heavens, we can remember that these kinds of supernatural modes of communication are not only part of fantasy stories. That which we see in the wizarding world of Harry Potter as merely magical is quite similar to the miraculous ways God has communicated with people so they could do their part to protect the Christ child and help carry out his mission.

The Muggle Protection Act

"Harry, that's their idea of fun. Half the Muggle killings back when You-Know-Who was in power were done for fun."

—Mr. Weasley, Book Four, p. 143

*I*n Book Three, Arthur Weasley introduced a Muggle Protection Act at the Ministry of Magic. Few details were provided, but those on Voldemort's side opposed this. Mr. Malfoy called Mr. Weasley a disgrace because of his desire to protect Muggles. Those on the side of good—Dumbledore, the Weasleys, Harry—share this love of Muggles. Mr. Weasley even tried to be kind to the Dursleys despite their rudeness to his family, mistrust, and outright meanness to Harry.

At the Quidditch World Cup, hooded Death Eaters attacked Muggles and threatened Muggle-born wizards. Mr. Weasley took immediate action to try to stop the attacks and catch the perpetrators. This concern for the welfare of Muggles shows a desire to protect them even though they are not in the wizarding world. Readers also see that those on the side of good do not discriminate against those who are of mixed blood or Muggle heritage, while many of the Slytherins and followers of Voldemort do.

The Muggle Protection Act can be seen as a parallel of how God loves the whole world, not just those who are already in the kingdom of God or even aware of the goings-on of the supernatural world. It reminds me of how Jesus treated the crowds of all sorts of people who came to him:

> Jesus went throughout Galilee, teaching in their synagogues and proclaiming the good news of the kingdom and curing every disease and every sickness among the people. So his fame spread throughout all Syria, and they brought to him all the sick, those who were afflicted with various diseases and pains, demoniacs, epileptics, and paralytics, and he cured them. And great crowds followed him from Galilee, the Decapolis, Jerusalem, Judea, and from beyond the Jordan. (Matt. 4:23–25)

These crowds were not just made up of those in the Jewish religious establishment. Indeed, these masses of humanity were made up of Gentiles (non-Jews), Samaritans (persons of Jewish heritage who worshiped on Mount Gerizim rather than Jerusalem), and people of various ethnic and religious backgrounds. This showed God's compassion for all people, even those who were not yet faithful to him or even fully aware of the spiritual battle Jesus was embroiled in while walking in their midst. "When he saw the crowds, he had compassion for them, because they were harassed and helpless, like sheep without a shepherd" (Matt. 9:36).

When we see how those on the side of good show compassion for the Muggles, let us call to mind the compassion of God for *all people* that is expressed in the life and ministry of Jesus Christ.

Mad-Eye Moody's Ironic Warnings

"A wizard who's about to put an illegal curse on you isn't going to tell you what he's about to do. He's not going to do it nice and polite to your face. You need to be prepared. You need to be alert and watchful."
—Mad-Eye Moody to Defense Against the
Dark Arts class, Book Four, p. 212

*M*ad-Eye Moody was introduced as a renowned fighter of evil, having put many of Voldemort's followers in prison. He is an auror, someone who sees what others miss, aided by his "mad eye" that can see all around and by other means, such as his foe glass, which warns him of approaching foes. His name also reveals that he was considered somewhat mad—good, but a bit mad. Throughout the greater part of Book Four, no one suspected that an evil impostor was merely replicating the real Mad-Eye Moody with the help of Polyjuice Potion.

"Professor Moody" taught his students about the three Unforgivable Curses: Cruciatus (pain), Imperius (total control), *Avada Kedavra* (instant death). These curses were presented as evil, extremely dangerous, and against the laws of the wizarding world. "Professor Moody" feigned not to promote these but to show the students how to protect themselves. He stressed that these must be resisted, saying, "That's what you're up against. That's what I have got to teach you to fight. You need preparing. You need arming. But most of all, you need to practice *constant, never-ceasing vigilance*" (Book Four, p. 217). In retrospect, the reader can see how ironic the lessons against the forbidden curses were. In reality, the one giving the lesson was fully devoted to Voldemort and to using these curses.

In the New Testament, Paul likewise warned his students when he was preparing to leave them, "I know that after I have gone, savage wolves will come in among you, not sparing the flock. Some even from your own group will come distorting the truth in order to entice the disciples to follow them. Therefore be alert, remembering that for three years I did not cease night or day to warn everyone with tears" (Acts 20:29–31).

The students in the third-year Defense Against the Dark Arts class taught by "Professor Moody" would have done well to note the nuances of such teaching, and so would we. The irony of Mad-Eye Moody's lesson on the need for constant vigilance is that he himself was an impostor they needed to be alert to detect. One wonders if Barty Crouch Jr., behind the facade of Mad-Eye Moody, got perverse pleasure out of such irony. He can serve to remind us that it is not enough to trust someone just because that person is part of some approved group or even in a position of authority.

What must be paramount in discerning good from evil is knowing the truth, not just deciding whether the one delivering the message seems trustworthy or not. The distortion of the truth is what we must guard against. Therefore, even in our world, when we know the truth about God revealed in the Bible, we can use that to discern whether any teaching is true, regardless of who delivers the message. It is far better, however, to receive a true message from someone who lives in keeping with the message proclaimed.

Luke was not a follower of Jesus when he lived on earth. Luke was more like an investigative reporter who became a disciple of Jesus after the resurrection. Then he made careful inquiry to record the truth about the life and teachings of Jesus. He begins his Gospel with this introduction:

Since many have undertaken to set down an orderly account of the events that have been fulfilled among us, just as they were handed on to us by those who from the beginning were eyewitnesses and servants of the word, I too decided, after investigating everything carefully from the very first, to write an orderly account for you, most excellent Theophilus, so that you may know the truth concerning the things about which you have been instructed. (Luke 1:1–4)

The record was set down after being carefully examined to see if it could be trusted as true. Even Jesus' opponents said to him, "Teacher, we know that you are right in what you say and teach, and you show deference to no one, but teach the way of God in accordance with truth" (Luke 20:21). However, one might detect a note of sarcasm in this comment since it was followed by a question meant to trap Jesus.

At the trial of Jesus, John relates the following exchange: "Pilate asked him, 'So you are a king?' Jesus answered, 'You say that I am a king. For this I was born, and for this I came into the world, to testify to the truth. Everyone who belongs to the truth listens to my voice.' Pilate asked him, 'What is truth?'" (John 18:37–38). Elsewhere, Jesus said of himself, "I am the way, and the truth, and the life. No one comes to the Father except through me" (John 14:6).

The whole weight of Jesus' ministry stands or falls on whether or not this statement he made about himself is true. If true, he is the *only* way to the Father, thus the only way to heaven. If this statement is not true, we dare not trust any of his claims or promises of eternal life. If this claim he made about himself is not true, he is shown to be a liar and a cruel impostor. Just as Barty Crouch Jr. impersonated a good teacher but was unmasked as an impostor, so too, if these statements by Jesus (and many of his other claims about himself) are not true, he cannot be called a good moral teacher.

Here is what C. S. Lewis had to say on this matter in his classic work, *Mere Christianity*:

I am trying here to prevent anyone saying the really foolish thing that people often say about Him: "I'm ready to accept Jesus as a great moral teacher, but I don't accept His claim to be God." That is the one thing we must not say. A man who was merely a man and said the sort of things Jesus said would not be a great moral teacher. He would either be a lunatic— on a level with the man who says he is a poached egg—or else he would be the Devil of Hell. You must make your choice. Either this man was, and is, the Son of God: or else a madman or something worse. You can shut Him up for a fool, you can spit at Him and kill Him as a demon; or you can fall at His feet and call Him Lord and God. But let us not come with any patronising nonsense about His being a great human teacher. He has not left that open to us. He did not intend to.[4]

As with Defense Against the Dark Arts at Hogwarts, knowing whether or not someone is an impostor is important. It is even more important that we know what truth is. Jesus made dramatic claims about who he is and why he came. If these are true, he deserves to be accepted as Messiah and worshiped as Lord and God; if they are not true, there is no place to call him a "good moral teacher" any more than one could rightly say that of Barty Crouch Jr.

The Only Known Survivor
of the Killing Curse

"There's no countercurse. There's no blocking it. Only one known person has ever survived it, and he's sitting right in front of me."
—Professor Moody to his Defense Against the
Dark Arts class, Book Four, p. 216

*H*arry is famous because he is the only known survivor of the Killing Curse. This has not been spelled out completely yet, but we do know that the key to Harry's survival was that his mother took the curse on herself and died in his place. Dumbledore said Voldemort could not understand such love. Tom Riddle seemed baffled by it when he quizzed Harry on how he had survived, wanting to know how a skinny boy like Harry "with no extraordinary magical talent" managed to defeat Voldemort and break his power. Harry replied that no one knew why Voldemort had lost his powers, but that he did know that the Dark Lord could not kill him because his mother had died to save him.

While Harry is the single survivor of the Killing Curse in these books—so far—the Bible actually has several stories that show how God sent a way of escape for impending death. When the people of Israel were warned that God was about to send a plague of death on the firstborn of the Egyptians, they were given a way to survive: "Thus says the LORD: 'About midnight I will go out through Egypt. Every firstborn in the land of Egypt shall die, from the firstborn of Pharaoh who sits on his throne to the first-born of the female slave who is behind the handmill, and all the firstborn of the livestock' " (Exod. 11:4–5). (Since this decree was made by God, it is not directly analogous to the Killing Curse used by Voldemort.) The only way to block this action was to put the blood of an unblemished male lamb on the doorposts and lintel of one's doorway. God said, "The blood shall be a sign for you on the houses where you live: when I see the blood, I will pass over you, and no plague shall destroy you when I strike the land of Egypt" (Exod. 12:13). God was true to his promise. Death passed over those homes covered by the blood of the Passover lamb. The celebration of Passover, which commemorates this, is a sacred celebration of this day for Jews, and many Christians incorporate elements of the Passover Seder in their traditions of worship.

The New Testament associates Passover with the death of Christ. When Jesus first began his ministry, John the Baptist announced him by saying, "Here is the Lamb of God who takes away the sin of the world!" (John 1:29). This signified that Jesus would die as the sacrificial lamb to pay for the sins of the people and make atonement for them. But it also relates Jesus to the Passover lamb. Indeed, Jesus died at Passover: "Now it was the day of Preparation for the Passover; and it was about noon. He said to the Jews, "Here is your King!" They cried out, "Away with him! Away with him! Crucify him!" (John 19:14–15). So, as it was prophesied, Jesus became our Passover lamb. All who apply the blood Jesus shed on the cross to the "door of their hearts" by faith will escape the "Killing Curse."

When Tom Riddle heard Harry say it was his mother's self-sacrificial death that saved him, he said, "Yes, that's a powerful counter-charm" (Book Two, p. 317). Likewise, the sacrifice of Jesus laying down his life to be our Passover lamb is a powerful way to counteract the curse of sin and death. In Harry's story, he is the only one so far who has been able to survive the fatal curse from the Dark Lord. We do not yet know if there will be some way for the whole wizarding world to take cover under some kind of "counter-charm" like the one that saved Harry, but the blood of

Jesus offers a way for everyone in our world to be protected from the curse of death.

The final outcome for all who escape the curse of death will be to stand triumphant before God, as death is destroyed once and forever:

And I heard a loud voice from the throne saying,

"See, the home of God is among mortals.
He will dwell with them as their God;
they will be his peoples,
and God himself will be with them;
he will wipe every tear from their eyes.
Death will be no more;
mourning and crying and pain will be no more,
for the first things have passed away."
(Rev. 21:3–4)

In our world, as in Harry's world, though some are safe, the Killing Curse still threatens many people. The Bible points us to a day when the curse of death will be destroyed entirely. We will have to wait and see what becomes of it in Harry's story.

Harry's Heroism in the Triwizard Tournament

> *"The Merchieftainess informs us that Mr. Potter was first to reach the hostages, and that the delay in his return was due to his determination to return all hostages to safety, not merely his own."*
>
> —Ludo Bagman, Book Four, p. 507

*T*he Triwizard Tournament consisted of three tasks. One was to get past a dragon, another to get through a maze, and another to rescue a hostage from under the lake. Harry was to rescue his friend, Ron; Fleur was to rescue her sister, Gabrielle; and Krum was to rescue Hermione. Harry got to the hostages first, and could have had a distinct advantage by saving Ron and moving on. But Harry was concerned about the safety of Hermione, because she was also his friend, and also Gabrielle, whom he barely knew. So Harry waited to make sure Krum got there to save Hermione, and then waited to see if Fleur was coming. When she did not show up, Harry rescued Gabrielle along with Ron. In doing so, he slowed himself down so much he missed the time limit.

In this act of heroism on Harry's part, we see his concern for all the hostages. He did not know what would happen to the hostages if they were not rescued, but he feared that they might die. He did know they could not save themselves. Fleur seemed to share Harry's concern that there was real danger for the hostages. When Harry saved her sister, she saw it as a gift of life for which she was ever grateful.

129

The Bible tells us that there will come a time when it is too late to be saved. God the Lord will return, the heavens and the earth will melt with intense heat (see 2 Pet. 3:3–7) and God will create a new heaven and a new earth in which righteousness will dwell (see Rev. 21:1). This has been predicted throughout human history. We do not know precisely when that time will come, but it will. The way Harry behaved under the lake reminds me of something the Bible tells us about why God has taken so long (in the opinion of some) to fulfill the promise of his return to set up the kingdom of heaven: Peter writes, "But do not ignore this one fact, beloved, that with the Lord one day is like a thousand years, and a thousand years are like one day. The Lord is not slow about his promise, as some think of slowness, but is patient with you, not wanting any to perish, but all to come to repentance" (2 Pet. 3:8–9).

So when we think about how Harry was slow in getting back out of the lake because of his concern to try to save all the hostages, we can bear in mind the patience of God and his love for all who are in danger of perishing eternally. We may not understand fully what that means, just as Harry could not be sure of the full consequences for the hostages under the lake, but we show true heroism when we do all we can to make sure those within our reach are saved.

The Daily Prophet:
News from the World Beyond

"Dumbledore!" cried Rita Skeeter, with every appearance of delight—but Harry noticed that her quill and the parchment had suddenly vanished.

—Book Four, p. 306–7

*I*n the wizarding world, people get their news from *The Daily Prophet,* a newspaper that employs reporters such as Rita Skeeter, with her Quick-Quotes Quill. Rita Skeeter reports the juicy gossip people love to read, she touches on real news stories, but pushes the truth aside for the sake of sensationalism. Readers of *The Daily Prophet* must be discerning to sift out the truth from that which is false or manipulated.

The Bible declares, "First of all you must understand this, that no prophecy of scripture is a matter of one's own interpretation, because no prophecy ever came by human will, but men and women moved by the Holy Spirit spoke from God" (2 Pet. 1:20–21). God has sent his message to our world from beyond by means of prophets and others who were moved by the Holy Spirit as they wrote down the Scripture. However, in an attempt to confuse God's message, the enemy has sent out many false prophets who proclaim and write what people want to hear and messages meant to confuse or contradict God's message. We are cautioned to be discerning whenever we hear a message that claims to be from God. The Bible declares itself to be the only true revelation of the will of God, by which we will be judged.

In our world, we read all kinds of reports and religious documents that claim to be messages from God, some about as reliable as Rita Skeeter's reporting. People argue over the Bible: Some declare it to be the true and infallible word of God, others are not so sure, still others scoff and try to discredit it. The Bible claims to be holy, which means set apart from all the rest, unique, the only true revelation of God. God says throughout his word that while he may add to his revelation during the formation of the canon of Scripture, we are not to add to his word, or take away from it. We see such warnings with the giving of God's law in Deuteronomy 4:2 and 12:32, in the wisdom of Proverbs 30:5–6, and in the last book of the New Testament, where it says: "I warn everyone who hears the words of the prophecy of this book: if anyone adds to them, God will add to that person the plagues described in this book; if anyone takes away from the words of the book of this prophecy, God will take away that person's share in the tree of life and in the holy city, which are described in this book" (Rev. 22:18–19). Obviously, if the Bible is God's holy word, this warning is not to be taken lightly.

What if the Bible is what it claims to be? Wouldn't it deserve at least as much attention and consideration as all the other sources of news and information that bombard us daily—things we read and watch that are less worthy of our consideration? If so, wouldn't it be a tragic success for the forces of evil if we became so confused or untrusting because of all the conflicting claims of the false prophets and Rita Skeeters of the world that we threw out the truth with the trivial?

Unlike *The Daily Prophet* in the wizarding world, the Bible is replete with fascinating elements that show the sincere seeker that it must be a true document sent by God from beyond. The unique qualities of the Bible are beyond mere human ingenuity and contradict mere human inclinations. Just the fulfilled prophecies alone are enough to substantiate its claims to be the authorized collection of God's message to humanity.

God appeals to this to cause us to see that he is the only one who could have written the Bible because it reveals much of human history before it has come to pass:

> I am the LORD, that is my name;
>   my glory I give to no other,
>   nor my praise to idols.
> See, the former things have come to pass,
>   and new things I now declare;
> before they spring forth,
>   I tell you of them.
>
> (Isa. 42:8–9)

Even though *The Daily Prophet* was less than reliable, people in Harry's world still read it and were influenced by it—often with negative results. Dare we disregard or neglect the one book that claims to contain the true and authorized messages from the world beyond through God's holy prophets?

The Death Eaters and the Dark Mark

"Every Death Eater had the sign burned into him by the
Dark Lord. It was a means of distinguishing one another,
and his means of summoning us to him."
—Professor Snape, Book Four, p. 710

Voldemort's followers, called Death Eaters, bore the Dark Mark on their bodies as a sign of allegiance to the Dark Lord. They openly followed him when he was in power, but after his downfall many claimed they had been acting against their will. Some were convicted and put in Azkaban. Many blended back into the wizarding population. Some worked at Hogwarts (noted for its firm stance against the Dark Arts), others worked at schools such as Durmstrang (that reportedly still taught the Dark Arts), and some even went to work at the Ministry of Magic.

At the Quidditch World Cup, someone projected the Dark Mark in the sky and called the Death Eaters to unify. Seeing this sign struck terror in the hearts of those who remembered the terrible times of the past. Then the Dark Mark would be projected over any place where someone had been murdered by the forces of the Dark Lord.

The Dark Mark was also used to call the Death Eaters to Voldemort whenever it became visible on their bodies. Both Karkaroff and Professor Snape had been troubled because the mark they bore had become more and more pronounced throughout the Triwizard Tournament. Neither intended to return; Karkaroff feared retribution because he had turned in many of his fellow Death Eaters, sending them to Azkaban so he could go free. Snape's full story has yet to come out, but we know he had been a Death Eater who renounced his involvement with Voldemort, made a turnaround and—somehow—gained Dumbledore's trust. Dumbledore even accepted him as a teacher at Hogwarts. However, his experience with the Dark Arts left its mark—which he can hide, but apparently not erase entirely.

When one thinks of a "Dark Mark" in biblical terms, one might recall "the mark of the beast," which Revelation says is a mark that will be put on those aligned with the antichrist before the last battle. However, there are significant differences that make a correlation between the Dark Mark and the mark of the beast only serve as a secondary parallel at best. There is another parallel that is more in keeping with the story line of the Harry Potter books, and goes more directly to the heart of the gospel. It calls us to focus our attention on Professor Snape. The Bible says,

> Do you not know that wrongdoers will not inherit the kingdom of God? Do not be deceived! Fornicators, idolaters, adulterers, male prostitutes, sodomites, thieves, the greedy, drunkards, robbers—none of these will inherit the kingdom of God. *And that is what some of you used to be. But you were washed, you were sanctified, you were justified* in the name of the Lord Jesus Christ and in the Spirit of our God. (1 Cor. 6:9–11)

This passage is a declaration that even those who have become known as one of the "wicked" in all their various classifications can become something different. This passage names all kinds of people and behaviors God says will disqualify one from the kingdom of God, then says "this is what some of you used to be. But . . ." It shows there is an opportunity for those who previously served the "Dark Lord" of our world to put their past behind them.

This passage declares: But you *were* washed. You *were* sanctified. You *were* justified. This declaration of acceptance regardless of one's past sinful classification leads into an understanding of the doctrines of absolution (washing), sanctification (being set apart as holy while God is at work transforming a person into one whose life is holy), and justification (being vindicated by God, declared not guilty).

The New Testament speaks of salvation as something that is simultaneously a done deal and an ongoing process. When people accept Christ as their new Lord, they are transferred instantly out of the kingdom of darkness and into the kingdom of God's Son. They are saved and sealed by the Holy Spirit, but they also begin a process of fully experiencing that salvation. God sees those who put their faith in Christ as already holy and blameless before him, while also calling them to progressively live lives marked outwardly by increasing holiness of character and conduct. This process of transformation involves being (1) washed: cleansed, having our past sins washed away, being absolved by God for what we have done; (2) sanctified: set apart by God as one of his own, but also the ongoing process of the working of the Word and the Spirit to equip us to serve God in the world and to live holy lives; and (3) justified: acquitted and vindicated by God, pronounced righteous (but not on the basis of what we have done; rather, on the basis of what Jesus did by dying on the cross to pay for our sins).

I am going to take a bit of a risk here by using Severus Snape and his relationship to Dumbledore as a parallel to how God works with those who have turned from allegiance to the Dark Lord of our world to join the ranks of those on God's side. This is a risk because we do not know what will become of Severus Snape in the Harry Potter stories. (I wonder if his name, Severus, might represent the fact that he severed his ties to the Dark Lord?) I believe the risk is worth taking because Dumbledore's treatment of Snape at this point in the book can be a good picture of a wonderful aspect of the gospel people often miss.

We know little about what Snape did while siding with Voldemort, except that he had been a Death Eater. But Dumbledore accepted Snape back, called him one of his own, and called on others to treat him as one who used to be but is no longer numbered among the Death Eaters. Somehow—and this is still unrevealed—Snape was absolved of former evildoing rather than being imprisoned. Dumbledore no longer sees him as a Death Eater or even just a former Death Eater, but as a trusted teacher at Hogwarts and a worthy ally of those on the good side.

Snape is one of the most curious of characters because it is not clear how or why Dumbledore would let one so dark in his demeanor be numbered on the side of good. Snape's sanctification can be seen in the way Dumbledore works with him, sometimes correcting him, sometimes calling him to serve him, sometimes calling him to make peace with old enemies. He has accepted him, but does not always accept the way he behaves. While he is treated as one who belongs fully to the good side, there are times Dumbledore must rein him in and even reprimand him. He works under Dumbledore's authority and ongoing supervision.

Perhaps the way Dumbledore deals with Snape could turn out to be a wonderful example of how God works with repentant sinners while transforming them into useful servants for his kingdom. In both cases, there are people in the process who do not seem to fit the image of someone on the side of good. In Christianity, all who trust Christ are called to holiness of life, but the actual transformation takes place from the inside out. So there are some people bearing the name of Christ who do not look the part, but we look on their outward appearance while God looks on the heart. We look at how they act now, while God looks at how far they have come from the wickedness they have left behind.

At some point, Dumbledore declared Snape justified, even though he used to be a Death Eater. The idea of being justified is a judicial concept. God is the ultimate judge. If he judged us just on the basis of what we have done—only by our "dark deeds"—no one could be justified. So in the Old Testament we see that David pleaded with God for mercy, knowing he was guilty of adultery and murder. He knew that God alone could free him from guilt, forgive his sins, and release him from the judgment he deserved (in that case, it was the death penalty). So when God punished David, but did not require the full death penalty, he was justified by God, even though acknowledged as a lawbreaker. In the New Testament, we are justified when God declares us "not guilty," because he has accepted Christ's crucifixion as payment and punishment for our sins. We do not know what the terms were between Dumbledore and Snape, but we do see that he has been justified somehow.

A character who is drawn in dark shades, like Snape, is the most likely kind of candidate to be thought of as what one might imagine a "sinner" or "wicked" person to be. So it is puzzling to see someone like Snape working at Hogwarts, even accepted and protected by Headmaster Dumbledore. Religious people have taken issue with the way God invites sinners to come to him. Indeed, Jesus said he came to call sinners to himself, not the righteous (or those who think of themselves as righteous). No matter how dark our past, how dark the stain our sins have left on our lives, or even how our sins have hurt others, there is a way back into God's good graces and a process of transformation that follows.

While sin will always have its consequences and leave a mark on us and our future, those who come back to God and repent can find assurance of God's acceptance, cleansing, sanctification, and justification. God can handle any "Dark Mark" for those who repent. This was prophesied by the prophet Isaiah:

> Come now, let us argue it out,
>   says the LORD:
> though your sins are like scarlet,
>   they shall be like snow;
> though they are red like crimson,
>   they shall become like wool.
> If you are willing and obedient,
>   you shall eat the good of the land;
> but if you refuse and rebel,
>   you shall be devoured by the sword;
>   for the mouth of the LORD has spoken.
>   (Isa. 1:18–20)

This was also promised in the New Testament: "If we confess our sins, he who is faithful and just will forgive us our sins and cleanse us from all unrighteousness. If we say that we have not sinned, we make him a liar, and his word is not in us" (1 John 1:9–10).

While still reserving final assessment of Severus Snape, I see the way Dumbledore treats him as a picture of hope for all who want to sever their ties with a past life of service to the Dark Lord of our world. There is hope for those who will come back to God and put the past away. They can receive absolution, a new position, and vindication. The one who is in authority over all our lives says we are not to indulge in the kinds of lifestyles that characterize those who will not enter the kingdom, but neither should we forget that such were some of us. The dark mark of our past does not have to brand our future.

The Wrath of Albus Dumbledore

There was no benign smile upon Dumbledore's face, no twinkle in the eyes behind the spectacles. There was cold fury in every line of the ancient face.
— Book Four, p. 679

Dumbledore realized that Mad-Eye Moody was an impostor when he removed Harry from the field against his orders. At that point, Dumbledore understood that there had been one in their midst with evil intentions, a consummate deceiver. He also knew Harry was in immediate danger. That is why he followed as soon as he was free of obligations. Just as Mad-Eye Moody's wand was poised to murder Harry, a blast of red blew away the door and downed the evil impostor. Dumbledore, Snape, and McGonagall had arrived just in time to save Harry. The fact that they appeared in the foe glass also revealed that whoever was in Moody's form was not on the side of good. The occasion allows Harry a chance to see another dimension to Dumbledore: "At that moment, Harry fully understood for the first time why people said Dumbledore was the only wizard Voldemort had ever feared. The look upon Dumbledore's face as he stared down at the unconscious form of Mad-Eye Moody was more terrible than Harry could have ever imagined" (Book Four, p. 679).

Dumbledore's wrath displayed in this situation was not contrary to his loving kindness and goodness; it was an appropriate display of it. In similar fashion, the images of God as both loving and at times full of wrath are not contradictory. The Bible presents a God who is loving, kind, long-suffering, patient, willing to forgive, and to reach out to every living soul. And yet, God's loving nature is also displayed in his hatred of evil. As we saw here, evil is that which comes to kill and destroy that which is good and those who are loved. Therefore, evil is hated, and those who cling to evil even after seeing the goodness of God will be subjected to his wrath.

We see this several places in the Old Testament, of which these passages are only a few:

> If you are willing and obedient,
>   you shall eat the good of the land;
> but if you refuse and rebel,
>   you shall be devoured by the sword;
> . for the mouth of the LORD has spoken.
> (Isa. 1:19–20)

> Hate evil and love good,
>   and establish justice in the gate.
> (Amos 5:15)

> Your arrows are sharp
>   in the heart of the king's enemies;
>   the peoples fall under you.
> Your throne, O God, endures forever and ever.
>   Your royal scepter is a scepter of equity;
>   you love righteousness and hate wickedness.
> Therefore God, your God, has anointed you
>   with the oil of gladness beyond your companions.
> (Ps. 45:5–7)

Isaiah's prophecy in chapter 61 is the messianic prophecy Jesus proclaimed himself to have fulfilled the day he spoke in the synagogue in Nazareth. Therein, Scripture puts God's love right alongside his vengeance, but notice that Jesus stopped short in his reading. Jesus read Isaiah's prophecy this far:

> The Spirit of the Lord is upon me,
>   because he has anointed me to bring good news to the poor.
> He has sent me to proclaim release to the captives

> and recovery of sight to the blind,
>   to let the oppressed go free,
> to proclaim the year of the Lord's favor.

(Luke 4:18–19)

Jesus stopped there—in mid-sentence—because his first coming was meant to offer the good news of God's love, comfort, and deliverance to the poor, the captives, and all who mourn. The sentence Jesus did not complete continues, "and the day of *vengeance* of our God . . ." (Isa. 61:2).

God's wrath is surrounded with his love and mercy, but to those who refuse and rebel, the wrath will be sure and severe. Therefore, the Bible says, "Let love be genuine; hate what is evil, hold fast to what is good" (Rom. 12:9). The wrath of Albus Dumbledore came out of his love for people and his commitment to hold fast to and protect that which was good.

The Bible clearly states, "For the wrath of God is revealed from heaven against all ungodliness and wickedness of those who by their wickedness suppress the truth" (Rom. 1:18). Barty Crouch Jr. acted as an impostor of one who was truly good, suppressing the truth with his Polyjuice Potion. He did so to carry out his wicked scheme to hand Harry over to Voldemort to be murdered, or to commit the murder himself. He deserved the wrath of Albus Dumbledore. Those on the good side did not have to fear such wrath; not so for those on the evil side.

Dumbledore waited for the Polyjuice Potion to wear off, knowing that when it did the identity of the deceiver would come to light. That brings to mind this bit of advice: "Let no one deceive you with empty words, for because of these things the wrath of God comes on those who are disobedient. Therefore do not be associated with them. For once you were darkness, but now in the Lord you are light" (Eph. 5:6–8).

Just as the wrath of Albus Dumbledore does not contradict his kindness or love, neither does the wrath of God contradict his. We must be careful not to be deceived by those who will rightly receive the wrath of God, and to make sure we live under the protection God provides so that we are not subject to his wrath.

Veritaserum: The Truth Will Be Told

*D*umbledore gave the impostor Veritaserum. It only took three drops to bring out the truth. He had no choice in the matter. Everything he had been hiding so deviously and for so long was revealed. This led to his condemnation.

The Bible tells us that God already knows everything. Everything we do, every idle word we speak, every thought—even the intent of our hearts is not hidden from God. However, we go through life trying to keep much hidden. The Bible makes it clear that the word of God is able to cut away all falsehood and get to the heart, to our most basic motives: "Indeed, the word of God is living and active, sharper than any two-edged sword, piercing until it divides soul from spirit, joints from marrow; it is able to judge the thoughts and intentions of the heart. And before him no creature is hidden, but all are naked and laid bare to the eyes of the one to whom we must render an account" (Heb. 4:12–13).

Barty Crouch Jr. had to give account to Dumbledore. Each human being will have to give account to God. As there was a "moment of truth" for Mr. Crouch, there will also be a specific moment when each of us will get the equivalent of Veritaserum and our secrets will become common knowledge. Hypocrites and impostors who have the most to hide also have the most to fear.

Consider what Jesus taught his disciples:

> Meanwhile, when the crowd gathered by the thousands, so that they trampled on one another, he began to speak first to his disciples, "Beware of the yeast of the Pharisees, that is, their hypocrisy. Nothing is covered up that will not be uncovered, and nothing secret that will not become known. Therefore whatever you have said in the dark will be heard in the light, and what you have whispered behind closed doors will be proclaimed from the housetops." (Luke 12:1–3)

While there will be a moment in the future when all the truth comes out, discretion must also be exercised wisely. In Book One, when Harry wanted to know the truth about some things, this was Dumbledore's reply: "'The truth.' Dumbledore sighed. 'It is a beautiful and terrible thing, and should therefore be treated with great caution'" (Book One, p. 298). Like Dumbledore, we should determine never to lie, but also be careful to handle the truth we know with consideration for the people to whom we would tell it. Like Harry, we do not know the whole truth yet, but we can be assured that one day it will all be revealed. On that day, those who have trusted the one who called himself "the truth" will be safe; those who have suppressed the truth in unrighteousness or tried to hide their evil deeds will be exposed and pay a terrible price similar to the price paid by Barty Crouch Jr.

The Kiss That Cost His Soul

He knew what the dementor must have done. It had administered its fatal kiss to Barty Crouch. It had sucked his soul out through his mouth. He was worse than dead.
                                        —Book Four, p. 703

*D*umbledore never wanted the dementors at Hogwarts. He certainly did not want them threatening his students. When Cornelius Fudge came into the room with a dementor, Professor McGonagall told him Dumbledore would never allow dementors to set foot inside the castle, but that did not stop him. The moment the dementor was in the room it swept down on Barty Crouch Jr. and administered the kiss. His expectations of honor from the Dark Lord were lost along with his soul.

The dementors had been described as soulless and evil creatures that sucked every good feeling and happy memory out of those they came near, leaving those under their influence too long with nothing but memories of the worst experiences of their lives. But the worst fate anyone could have was to receive the dementor's kiss, which left the person technically alive but without his or her soul. Harry was right in thinking this was a fate worse than death. Even though Dumbledore dealt severely with Barty Crouch Jr., he did not want him to lose his soul.

The Bible and the Harry Potter stories agree that there is something worse than death. When God created human beings he gave them a soul, that part of them destined for eternity and capable of loving or rejecting him. The eternal soul of every person will either enjoy the blessings and comforts of God's presence forever or be lost in a tortured eternity apart from God. Everyone will die, seeing that mortality is part of the curse that came on humanity because of sin. But, compared to physical death, the loss of one's soul is far more important than when or how one dies. No earthly power or material wealth can compare to the worth of a human soul. As Jesus asked, "What good is it for a man to gain the whole world, yet forfeit his soul? Or what can a man give in exchange for his soul?" (Mark 8:36–37 NIV). This is repeated in three of the four Gospels.

Jesus never gave his disciples a guarantee of protection from pain, hardship, or death; indeed, he predicted that they would suffer and that some would be put to death because of their testimony about him. He did emphasize that the final and eternal destiny of each human soul is of far greater importance than temporary troubles in this life. The Bible says, "For this slight momentary affliction is preparing for us an eternal weight of glory far beyond all measure" (2 Cor. 4:17).

The fear and revulsion over the dementor's kiss can remind us of the gravity of one lost soul—even one as despicable as Barty Crouch Jr. Whenever the dementor's kiss is dealt with in Harry's world, it is always treated as worse than death. This is how the Bible treats the loss of one soul.

Jesus clearly rated death a distant second to the risk of losing one's soul. He told his disciples, "Do not fear those who kill the body but cannot kill the soul; rather fear him who can destroy both soul and body in hell" (Matt. 10:28). The Bible teaches that there is a real hell, which was created for the devil and his angels—never for human beings. Therefore, Jesus personally does everything he can to dissuade people from going to hell. Consider the story Jesus tells in Luke 16:19–31 of the rich man who learned too late of the power and permanence of hell. Jesus ended this story with a sad prophecy of what he could foresee. Even after he rose from the dead, there would still be those who would not listen to his warnings. But he made sure we had these warnings while there is still time for our souls to be rescued.

Just as Dumbledore took no delight in seeing even an evil man receive the dementor's kiss, God takes no delight in seeing any soul be lost and cast into hell. Jesus never made light of hell; instead he showed his urgent concern for and desire to save those whose souls were in danger.

> What man among you, if he has a hundred sheep and has lost one of them, does not leave the ninety-nine in the open pasture, and go after the one which is lost, until he finds it? And when he has found it, he lays it on his shoulders, rejoicing. And when he comes home, he calls together his friends and his neighbors, saying to them, "Rejoice with me, for I have found my sheep which was lost!" I tell you that in the same way, there will be more joy in heaven over one sinner who repents, than over ninety-nine righteous persons who need no repentance. (Luke 15:3–7 NASB)

In reflecting on the kiss that cost a man his soul, consider the contrast of emotions at the end of Book Four as compared to the end of Book Three when Harry and Sirius Black both escaped the dementor's kiss. The dementor's kiss brought tragedy and solemn trepidation with no hope for the future. Rescue from the dementor's kiss brought exhilarating relief, comfort, and joy shared by Harry, Sirius, and all who loved them (along with expectations for a good future). That is like the contrast of emotions we feel toward the rich man in Jesus' parable who faced eternity in torment, as compared to the relief and joy we feel for the poor man in the story Jesus told who ended up in the afterlife comforted and celebrating with Abraham for all eternity.

The Parting of the Ways

"If your determination to shut your eyes will carry you as far as this, Cornelius," said Dumbledore, *"we have reached a parting of the ways. You must act as you see fit. And I—I shall act as I see fit."*

—Book Four, p. 709

Cornelius Fudge, Minister of Magic, reacted to the confessions of Barty Crouch Jr. and news of Voldemort's return in a very strange way. He sought to deny it and discredit the evidence. By allowing the dementor to administer its kiss, he effectively got rid of the star witness. His reaction toward Dumbledore revealed that he was unwilling to stand with him against evil. This is what brought them to a parting of the ways.

Fudge refused to believe the story Barty Crouch Jr. had told under the compulsion of Veritaserum (or perhaps just refused to admit it openly). Instead, he characterized Crouch as a lunatic murderer. He rejected the assembled testimony of trustworthy witnesses (Harry, Dumbledore, Snape, and McGonagall) who had no reason to lie or make up such a story. Even if they did want to concoct such a story, they could not have been so clever as to come up with a story that made sense of all the details and be able to agree on a cohesive story line with so little time to form a conspiracy. Fudge also swept aside or disregarded the mute evidence of Snape's Dark Mark that had appeared on his arm. Most significantly, he made no attempt to deal with the reality of Cedric's murder: that the boy's dead body had no mark was clear evidence that he had been the victim of the Killing Curse. If he wanted to go further, he could have sought to verify

Barty Crouch Jr.'s testimony by exhuming the bone (that had once been the body of Mr. Crouch Sr.). But he did none of this.

Cornelius Fudge openly admitted that he did not *want* to believe their testimony because it would upset the status quo and threaten his political position. If the story as told by Harry and the others was true, it reflected poorly on some people with whom Fudge had aligned himself (and could possibly uncover other things Fudge may be hiding, which remain hidden at this point in the story). We do know that Harry could name the Death Eaters who returned to Voldemort at his call, those he saw in the graveyard. These included MacNair, whom Fudge had hired to work at the Ministry, and Lucius Malfoy, who held considerable power; Fudge had vouched for both of them. Rather than upset all of that, Fudge exhibited a determination to shut his eyes. Therefore, Dumbledore declared they had reached a parting of the ways.

Cornelius Fudge tried to turn this around to make it look like Dumbledore was setting himself against him (and, by inference, the Ministry), but he was set straight. "'The only one against whom I intend to work,' said Dumbledore, 'is Lord Voldemort. If you are against him, then we remain, Cornelius, on the same side'" (Book Four, p. 709).

Even though Dumbledore was open to all and accepted those whose loyalties were questionable while Voldemort was in hiding, there came a time when all had to declare their allegiance. There was no longer middle ground, no wiggle room with regard to which side one was on. This is similar to the progression of Jesus' ministry. He called the crowds to him, including those who were questionable or uncertain of their position with regard to God and himself. However, a time came when everyone had to declare whether they were with Jesus or against him:

> John said to him, "Teacher, we saw someone casting out demons in your name, and we tried to stop him, because he was not following us." But Jesus said, "Do not stop him; for no one who does a deed of power in my name will be able

soon afterward to speak evil of me. Whoever is not against us is for us. For truly I tell you, whoever gives you a cup of water to drink because you bear the name of Christ will by no means lose the reward." (Mark 9:38–41)

At another time Jesus was being accused by the religious leaders of casting out demons by the power of Satan (aka: Beelzebul). Jesus countered with this:

> If Satan also is divided against himself, how will his kingdom stand?—for you say that I cast out the demons by Beelzebul. Now if I cast out the demons by Beelzebul, by whom do your exorcists cast them out? Therefore they will be your judges. But if it is by the finger of God that I cast out the demons, then the kingdom of God has come to you. . . . Whoever is not with me is against me, and whoever does not gather with me scatters. (Luke 11:18–23)

Jesus and the religious leaders who refused to believe in him had reached a parting of the ways. Not unlike Cornelius Fudge, the religious leaders Jesus confronted had a lot to lose if Jesus were truly what he proclaimed himself to be—Son of God, Son of Man, Son of David, "I Am"—which adds up to Messiah. They had worked their whole lives to attain the positions he could make obsolete. Besides, his claims were sure to create conflict with their Roman governors, which would cause an uprising that might rightly be feared. The Roman way of dealing with such uprisings was brutal, and many would surely die. Besides, their entire political and religious establishment would be destroyed. They opted to shut their eyes because of the implications the truth could have for their own lives.

There will be a parting of the ways when everyone will have to choose sides. Jesus stated it this way: "Everyone therefore who acknowledges me before others, I also will acknowledge before my Father in heaven; but whoever denies me before others, I also will deny before my Father in heaven" (Matt. 10:32–33). Before we arrive at that parting of the ways, we would do well to see where we stand and whether any determination to shut our eyes might have more to do with the implications of what we might see rather than the reliability of the evidence and testimony of eyewitnesses recorded in the Bible.

We Are Only as Strong
as We Are United

*"Time is short, and unless the few of us who know the truth
. . . stand united, there is no hope for any of us."*
—Dumbledore to Professor Snape and
Sirius Black, Book Four, p. 712

As Professor Dumbledore sought to consolidate the ranks of those ready to oppose Voldemort, he had to bring together some who were openly hostile to each other. Sirius Black and Severus Snape were called on to lay aside their old differences, or at least call a truce, as Dumbledore pronounced them to be on the same side. If they did not stand together, they would not be able to stand at all. In the Great Hall, Dumbledore told the assembly,

> I say to you all, once again—in the light of Lord Voldemort's return, we are only as strong as we are united, as weak as we are divided. Lord Voldemort's gift for spreading discord and enmity is very great. We can fight it only by showing an equally strong bond of friendship and trust. Differences of habit and language are nothing at all if our aims are identical and our hearts are open. (Book Four, p. 723)

Unity is at the heart of the gospel, although this is often not apparent in the ranks of those who share a belief in the Bible, even among those who have a shared faith in Jesus as their Messiah. This is not unlike what we see in the ranks of those Dumbledore is assembling. Jesus made it clear that this call for unity was not

151

something new, but was at the heart of the Old Testament declaration of the very nature of God:

> One of the scribes came near and heard them disputing with one another, and seeing that he answered them well, he asked him, "Which commandment is the first of all?" Jesus answered, "The first is, 'Hear, O Israel: the Lord our God, *the Lord is one;* you shall love the Lord your God with all your heart, and with all your soul, and with all your mind, and with all your strength.' The second is this, 'You shall love your neighbor as yourself.' There is no other commandment greater than these." (Mark 12:28–31)

Jesus' final prayer for his followers, in John 17:1–26, was a primarily a prayer for unity and protection from the evil one: "I ask you to protect them from the evil one. . . . I ask not only on behalf of these, but also on behalf of those who will believe in me through their word, that they may all be one" (John 17:15, 20–21). This prayer shows that unity among his followers was of utmost importance to Jesus.

The evil one warned against in the Bible has—as Dumbledore phrased it—"a gift for spreading discord and enmity." Therefore, the Bible warns against the things that disrupt unity:

> Live by the Spirit, I say, and do not gratify the desires of the flesh. For what the flesh desires is opposed to the Spirit, and what the Spirit desires is opposed to the flesh. . . . Now the works of the flesh are obvious: fornication, impurity, licentiousness, idolatry, sorcery, enmities, strife, jealousy, anger, quarrels, dissensions, factions, envy, drunkenness, carousing, and things like these. I am warning you, as I warned you before: those who do such things will not inherit the kingdom of God. (Gal. 5:16–21)

In our world—as in Harry's—those who know the truth need to put aside old differences and stand united, thereby building up friendship and trust. When we do, we will act in unity with God and each other. Then the power of God can flow through us uninterrupted to accomplish God's will on earth as it is in heaven.

What Will Come, Will Come

*"Known it fer years, Harry. Knew he was out there bidin'
his time. It had ter happen. Well, now it has, an we'll jus'
have ter get on with it. We'll fight. Migh' be able ter stop
him before he gets a good hold."*
— Hagrid to Harry, Ron, and Hermione,
Book Four, p. 719

Although the coming battle is unwelcome, Hagrid knew it was inevitable. Voldemort is evil, and evil is aggressive. It seeks to overpower good, and therefore seeks to destroy all that is good. Dumbledore and those opposing Voldemort will not—dare not— step aside and let evil overtake their world. They knew that Voldemort had not been destroyed utterly. They had seen his schemes being worked out in various ways, through various willing and unwilling accomplices. It was only a matter of time until there had to be an outright battle. Everyone will be forced to declare allegiance either to Voldemort's side or Dumbledore's side. Book Four ends with Harry thinking, "As Hagrid had said, what would come, would come . . . and he would have to meet it when it did" (Book Four, p. 734).

Anyone can look at our world and know that evil is still lurking out there. The Bible is quite clear in warning us that evil will not sit idle, but is biding its time.

The battle between good and evil is ongoing, in the everyday struggles of each human soul and as evidenced in any nightly news broadcast. However, beyond this, the Bible predicts a time when Satan (the evil one) and all the forces of evil will rise up to make a final challenge against God and those who align themselves on the side of good. History also teaches us that evil tyrants do not sit idle when they are out of power, although they may have to bide their time while awaiting an opportune moment to attack. Like Voldemort, evil tyrants, despots, terrorists, and would-be dictators all lie in wait, unseen, while planning their rise to power. They too resolve to destroy whoever gets in their way, with murderous intent and without remorse. Therefore, no matter how comfortable we feel, we would do well to bear in mind that evildoers are always lurking out there somewhere in the world, planning, plotting, and biding their time. This awareness will help us not be caught unprepared.

As Dumbledore prepared his side for battle, Jesus similarly prepared his disciples to expect that there would be battles to be fought. But he also sought to ease their fears:

> When you hear of wars and revolutions, do not be frightened. These things must happen first, but the end will not come right away.
>   Then he said to them: "Nation will rise against nation, and kingdom against kingdom. There will be great earthquakes, famines and pestilences in various places, and fearful events and great signs from heaven." (Luke 21:9–11 NIV)

There are battles left to be fought: skirmishes in moral and political realms, "wars and rumors of wars," ethnic groups rising up to destroy other ethnic groups, nations rising up against nations. However, we are not to give in to fear, but rather to make sure that we take our stand on the side of good. In every battle between good and evil, within ourselves and in every earthly struggle, we too must choose sides carefully. With God's guidance, we can determine good from evil, dare to do that which is good, and bravely resist evil, regardless of the cost. But that is not the whole of the story.

The Bible gives us the advantage of knowing how to live intent on overcoming evil, but also assures us that the ultimate war between good and evil will be won by those on the side of good. In the face of the aggressive nature of evil, we are told, "Do not be overcome by evil, but overcome evil with good" (Rom. 12:21). The positive is to actively overcome the negative.

The Bible also tells us how:

> Be on guard so that your hearts are not weighed down with dissipation and drunkenness and the worries of this life, and that day catch you unexpectedly, like a trap. For it will come upon all who live on the face of the whole earth. Be alert at all times, praying that you may have the strength to escape all these things that will take place, and to stand before the Son of Man. (Luke 21:34–36)

In the Harry Potter series, Book Four ends in the middle of the larger story. As with most good stories, we are left hanging at a crisis point and do not know how the remaining battles will end. However, in our world, while acknowledging the ongoing battles between good and evil, the Bible tells us that we can look forward to a wonderful end. (I am expecting a positive outcome in Harry's world too.)

In Harry's world, Hagrid can face the battle to come with courage because he knows Dumbledore will be leading them: "Great man, Dumbledore. 'S long as we've got him, I'm not too worried" (Book Four, p. 719). God consoles us with the assurance that God is always with us, that the Holy Spirit is our comforter, and that whenever two or three gather in Jesus' name, he will be with us. So we have assurance that whatever battles we face, we are not alone and we are not helpless.

The Bible also gives us a "blessed hope" that a day will come when Jesus will return to earth physically to defeat the forces of evil in a final battle. It also tells us how to live until that day:

> For the grace of God that brings salvation has appeared to all men. It teaches us to say "No" to ungodliness and worldly passions, and to live self-controlled, upright and godly lives in this present age, while we wait for the blessed hope—the glorious appearing of our great God and Savior, Jesus Christ,

who gave himself for us to redeem us from all wickedness and to purify for himself a people that are his very own, eager to do what is good. (Titus 2:11–14 NIV)

In our world—as in the wizarding world of Harry Potter—what is coming will come, and we will have to face it when it does. However, there is good news that counteracts the evil that remains active in our world. The Bible assures us that Jesus will come back. When he does, he will crush all the forces of evil and overcome evil with good forever! The promised return of Jesus, the Prince of Peace, is a bright opposite to the ominous expectation of the Dark Lord's return in Harry's world. Humanity does have to face the reality that there are battles left to be fought and won against evil in our world. While we must be vigilant, we can rest assured in "the blessed hope" that the One who is coming will come, and we can look forward to meeting him when he does.

Dumbledore Welcomes All
Who Wish to Come

"Every guest in this Hall," said Dumbledore, and his eyes lingered upon the Durmstrang students, "will be welcomed back here at any time, should they wish to come."
—Book Four, p. 723

Book Four ends with Voldemort having acquired human form, by force and dark magic. With the bone of the father he murdered, the flesh of one of his servants, and the blood of his enemy, the Dark Lord rose again. Dumbledore took his stand against him, and invited all to stand with him on the side of good. He called together the Hogwarts students and students who had been visiting from other wizarding schools for the Triwizard Tournament. He reminded them that they were always welcome in his banquet hall. His eyes lingered on the Durmstrang students, perhaps because Durmstrang was one of the schools that still taught some of the Dark Arts. Dumbledore wanted those students in particular to know that they could still choose good even if they had been schooled in evil.

Dumbledore had distinguished himself as one who extended open arms even to those others rejected. He excluded no one because of what they were, what had happened to them, what they were believed to be, or what they had done, if they were willing to turn away from evil. He had shown his open arms policy many times. He hired Professor Lupin, who was a werewolf. He hired Hagrid, even though he had been falsely convicted of opening the Chamber of Secrets and was obviously half-giant. He hired Professor Snape, even though he had once been a Death Eater. He

157

invited schools to the Triwizard Tournament that had questionable leaders (Karkaroff had been a Death Eater, and Madam Maxime appeared to be part giant). He hired Filch, who was a squib (having magical parentage, but no apparent magical powers), and Gilderoy Lockhart, whose credentials were bogus. So Dumbledore's track-record of welcoming all who would come backed up his invitation.

The Bible lays out a panoramic battle between good and evil, God and Satan, and people are caught in the midst of this battle whether they like it or not. Such is the nature of human life. The battle began before we were born, and we each must end up on a side, whether by choice or default. But God sent us a message to let us know we are all welcome on his side under his protection, or—figuratively—in his banquet hall.

Jesus told a story about a fictional king who gave a wedding banquet for his son. But all the people originally invited refused to come. Again, the king sent out his servants to tell them that he had a wonderful feast planned for them, that they were wanted and welcome, but they made light of it and again declined his invitation to the banquet. Some simply went about their daily business, which they deemed more important, while others abused and killed the king's servants who delivered the invitation. So the king sent troops and killed those who had murdered his messengers. (Given the importance of the king and the villainous response of those invited, this was considered an appropriate response. Such a flagrant refusal to receive a king's hospitality was a dishonor to the royal family.) "Then he said to his slaves, 'The wedding is ready, but those invited were not worthy. Go therefore into the main streets, and invite everyone you find to the wedding banquet.' Those slaves went out into the streets and gathered all whom they found, both good and bad; so the wedding hall was filled with guests" (Matt. 22:8–10). This follows with a scene of the king arriving to find that one of the welcomed guests did not dress appropriately for the banquet and was therefore tossed out, but all the others—both good and bad—enjoyed the king's hospitality.

This parable was Jesus' way of speaking to the Jewish religious leaders of his day who knew the Scriptures and the prophecies of the Messiah. They had been the first to receive God's invitation to honor his Son. The religious elite were the ones represented as refusing the invitation and killing the king's messengers. They were the real villains of the story. Elsewhere, he accused them of masquerading as good, and referred to them as whitewashed tombs. So Jesus' story meant that God was done with them. They had come to a parting of the ways. Soon Roman troops would overthrow them and destroy the temple.

At the tail end of this sober warning for those who should have received the invitation but refused, there came good news for everybody else. God's banquet hall and lavish feast was now wide open to any and all who wished to come. Granted, those who did choose to come needed to dress appropriately, spiritually speaking (in the "robes of righteousness" provided for them) in order to stay.

In our world, we see the open arms of God when Jesus called for all who were weary and heavy laden to come to him, when he called for all who were thirsty to come to him, when all who were sick or possessed by demons came to him and were healed, when he called the little children to come to him and then picked them up in his arms and blessed them. God's arms were extended to everyone when Jesus sent his disciples out into all the world to preach the gospel of God's love.

John writes of Jesus,

> He was in the world, and the world came into being through him; yet the world did not know him. He came to what was his own, and his own people did not accept him. But *to all who received him,* who believed in his name, he gave power to become children of God, who were born, not of blood or of the will of the flesh or of the will of man, but of God. (John 1:10–13)

Peter extended this invitation to a crowd assembled in Jerusalem: "Repent, and be baptized *every one of you* in the name of

Jesus Christ so that your sins may be forgiven; and you will receive the gift of the Holy Spirit. *For the promise is for you, for your children, and for all who are far away, everyone whom the Lord our God calls to him*" (Acts 2:38–39). God's invitation is not limited to a select guest list but is open to all: "For there is no distinction between Jew and Greek; the same Lord is Lord of all and is generous to all who call on him. For, 'Everyone who calls on the name of the Lord shall be saved'" (Rom. 10:12–13).

Albus Dumbledore's reminder to all the students, good and bad alike, that they are welcome back any time they wish to come reflects God's open arms and warm welcome to all who are willing to respond positively to his invitation.

Afterword

I began this book while looking at white clouds against a brilliant blue sky and reflecting on how they awakened my imagination and that of my kids. Metaphorically, this book goes from a bright sky on a spring day to a point midway through the Harry Potter series that might rightly be likened to dark clouds overshadowing the wizarding world. The end of Book Four leaves us at the darkest point, looking forward to an inevitable battle. We know there are three more books to follow, but we are left with much that is uncertain. We wonder where it will lead: What terrible things will happen? Who will live and who will die?

If this book simply looked at the themes of the Harry Potter stories, it might be appropriate to let it end under a darkened sky too. However, since this is a book about the gospel—God's *good news*—as it relates to Harry Potter, we do not have to end on a dark note. There is an appropriate gospel parallel that takes up where the story left off.

Imagine yourself as being alive during the time of Jesus. For this purpose, it makes little difference whether you would most aptly see yourself as a curious bystander, a skeptic, a seeker, a devoted disciple, or even an avowed enemy of Jesus. Imagine yourself in Jerusalem on the day of his crucifixion. You see him publicly condemned to death, beaten mercilessly, ridiculed, mocked, pushed along up that dusty hill that forms the shape of a skull. You hear the crack of wood and iron as the mallet pounds the nails through human flesh, and the attendant screams of the three men being crucified that day. The spectacle gets underway at about nine in the morning, then at noon an ominous darkness covers the entire sky. The Gospel of Luke describes it this way:

161

> It was now about the sixth hour, and darkness came over the whole land until the ninth hour, for the sun stopped shining. And the curtain of the temple was torn in two. Jesus called out with a loud voice, "Father, into your hands I commit my spirit." When he had said this, he breathed his last.
>
> The centurion, seeing what had happened, praised God and said, "Surely this was a righteous man." When all the people who had gathered to witness this sight saw what took place, they beat their breasts and went away. But all those who knew him, including the women who had followed him from Galilee, stood at a distance, watching these things. (Luke 23:44–49)

The darkness at midday gave way to a hurried burial and to a dark night in which no one in Jerusalem could celebrate an untroubled Passover. However, they did not have to wait years for the rest of the story! At daybreak on the third day, the sun arose with a brilliance that was put to shame only by the brilliance of the angels who announced that Jesus had risen from the dead just as he promised. The curse was indeed broken! All who would believe in him, trusting that he had taken the curse of death in their place, would live eternally.

Before he died, Jesus had told his disciples that he must go up to Jerusalem, be given over into the hands of evil men, suffer many things, be crucified, die, and be buried. Then on the third day he would rise from the dead. Apparently his disciples thought this was some sort of literary metaphor. But the predictions Jesus made were not a flight of fantasy. His resurrection confirmed that he had foretold a glorious reality.

Everyone who heard the glad tidings and curious rumors about his resurrection had to decide what to believe about the stories he had told, the claims he had made, and the man who claimed to be the one and only Son of God. Even the disciples had to think it all through again in the fresh light of his resurrection. What did it all mean now? What about Jesus' warnings that some of them would die because of their testimony about him before kings and governors? What of all the other stories they may have taken as fantasy or metaphor—could those be real too? What of all his promises, predictions, warnings—what did all that he had taught mean for them and the future of the human race?

Jesus stayed with them for forty days, appearing and disappearing (or *disapparating,* as they would say in Harry's world). One time he appeared to over five hundred witnesses at once. He taught his disciples many things regarding the kingdom of God. That kingdom of God had arrived and they were part of it, although it was invisible to most. That kingdom had come, but it was also yet to come. Jesus was going away to prepare a place for them, but he would return to earth to fight one last battle when he would destroy the forces of evil entirely. The disciples were told to wait in Jerusalem until they received power from on high when the Holy Spirit would come upon them. Then they would use that power to be his witnesses to the ends of the earth and until the end of time. Then Jesus went back up into heaven, ascending before their eyes until the clouds obscured him from their sight.

I like the idea of leaving you looking up at the clouds, where we began. But I also want to reprise Albus Dumbledore's invitation. You may have picked up this book for any number of reasons, perhaps the least of which was to seek God or actually hear the gospel. I wrote this book for several reasons, but one was to extend God's welcoming invitation to you. I particularly hoped that some would really hear the gospel who had never heard it before, perhaps because they were turned off by the way it has been presented.

Another reason I wrote this book was to challenge my fellow Christians to think again about the Harry Potter books. Many non-Christians share my discomfort with the fact that many critics of Harry Potter have never read even one of the four books for themselves. It is hard to be adamant if you choose to remain personally ignorant by relying only on impressions and hearsay without reading the story in question for yourself.

I find it an interesting parallel that many who have neglected or rejected the gospel have done so without actually reading even one of the four Gospels for themselves. Whatever conclusions they have come to are also based on impressions, hearsay, and second-hand accounts. All seekers of truth owe it to themselves to read at least one of the four Gospels. (For a free copy of the Gospel of John, contact The Pocket Testament League at 1-800-636-8785 or www.readcarryshare.org.)

I hope you enjoyed this alternative look at Harry Potter. We live at a time when the battle between evil and good is growing intense; sides are being drawn up even still. As we face our own battles and dark days ahead, let us remember that good will triumph over evil and that God's arms are open wide, his banquet hall is open to us all, and he welcomes all who wish to come.

Notes

1. Kurt Bruner and Jim Ware, *Finding God in Lord of the Rings* (Wheaton, Ill.: Tyndale House Publishers, 2001), 110.

2. From Thomas L. Martin, "Lewis: A Critical Perspective," in *Reading the Classics with C .S. Lewis,* ed. Thomas L. Martin, (Grand Rapids: Baker Academic, 2000), 277. "By the year 1931, Lewis came from the idea of myth as a mere falsehood to the belief that Christianity is a 'true myth' verified by a historical 'fact,' whereas Pagan myths chiefly remain products of human imagination. Their origins are vague and mixed: 'in the huge mass of mythology which has come down to us a good many different sources are mixed—true history, allegory, ritual, the human delight in story-telling, etc. But among these sources I include the supernatural, both diabolical and divine'" ("Religion Without Dogma?" in *Undeceptions: Essays on Theology and Ethics.* [London: Geoffrey Books, 1971], 99–114). Thus, Lewis came to believe that "at its best" myth is "a real though unfocused gleam of divine truth falling on human imagination" (*Miracles: A Preliminary Study* [London: Collins, 1966]).

3. Josh McDowell, *The New Evidence That Demands a Verdict* (Nashville: Thomas Nelson, 1999); Lee Strobel, *The Case for Christ* (Grand Rapids: Zondervan, 1998).

4. C. S. Lewis, *Mere Christianity* (San Francisco: HarperSanFrancisco, 2001), 52.

Acknowledgments

*M*y sincere appreciation goes to the following people:

Mark I. Pinsky, author of *The Gospel according to The Simpons,* sparked the idea of addressing Harry Potter in this context while interviewing me for the *Orlando Sentinel*. Thanks, Mark! Not all of my intereactions with the media are as fruitful.

David Dobson, senior editor, had enthusiasm for this book from the beginning, which blossomed into a very positive collaborative effort.

John W. Morehead of Watchman Fellowship reviewed the manuscript with an eye toward any theological statements that might be perceived to fall outside the bounds of biblical orthodoxy. Hopefully his expertise, careful theological review, and the excellent reputation of the Watchman Fellowship will help some who might otherwise hesitate to fully enjoy this book.

Julie Tonini and the production team at Westminster John Knox Press did a fine job of editing. The creative process employed in this kind of writing requires the balance of good editing. Their careful work clarified my intentions and made the book far more enjoyable to read.

Dr. David George, pastor, and the community at Valley Springs Presbyterian Church provided the spiritual base our family needs to grow in our love for God as well as an appreciation for literature and the arts. The fun, enthusiastic spiritual discussions we had in our "Harry Potter Book Club and Bible Study" showed me how much there was to develop from these stories. My special thanks to **the James family (especially Charlotte, Beth, and Martha) and my daughter, Haley,** for their continued participation and encouragement.

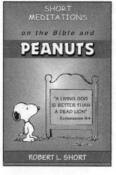

Did You Enjoy This Book?

Connie Neal's other books and resources can be found at www.ConnieNeal.com.
These include a complete resource kit for churches and religious schools to help them
handle Harry Potter in a positive and biblical way. For speaking engagements with
Connie Neal, please contact Susan Yates at (714) 285-9540.

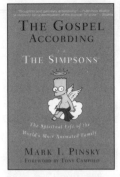

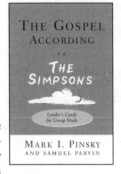